GROWTH

training
vs. trying

ROWTH

raining
vs. trying

JOHN ORTBERG
LAURIE PEDERSON
JUDSON POLING

PURSUING SPIRITUAL TRANSFORMATION

ZONDERVAN™
GRAND RAPIDS, MICHIGAN 49530 USA

WILLOW
Willow Creek Resources

ZONDERVAN.COM/
AUTHORTRACKER

ZONDERVAN™

Growth: Training vs. Trying
Copyright © 2000 by the Willow Creek Association

Requests for information should be addressed to:
Zondervan, *Grand Rapids, Michigan 49530*

ISBN-10: 0-310-22075-0
ISBN-13: 978-0-310-22075-6

We are grateful for permission given by a number of gifted teachers to use excerpts from their books and messages for the opening readings in the sessions. These authors and speakers are acknowledged throughout this guide.

Interior design by Laura Klynstra Blost

Printed in the United States of America

09 10 /❖ EP/ 25

CONTENTS

Pursuing Spiritual Transformation

The Pursuing Spiritual Transformation series is all about being spiritual. But that may not mean what you think!

Do you consider yourself a spiritual person? What does that mean? Does spiritual growth seem like an impossible amount of work? Do you have a clear picture of the kind of life you'd live if you were to be more spiritual?

Each guide in the Pursuing Spiritual Transformation series is dedicated to one thing—helping you pursue authentic spiritual transformation. Here, the focus is learning to train for growth.

You may find this study different from others you have done in the past. Each week in preparation for your group meeting, you will be completing a Bible study and experimenting with a variety of spiritual exercises. These elements are designed to enhance your private times with God and, in turn, to help you invite him into all aspects of your life, even the everyday routines. After all, spiritual life is just *life*—the one you live moment by moment.

It is very important that you complete this work before going to each meeting because the discussion is based on what you've learned from the study and what you've observed as a result of the spiritual exercise. The Bible study and exercises are not meant to be done an hour before the meeting, quickly filling in the blanks. Instead, we suggest you thoughtfully and prayerfully complete them over the course of several days as part of your regular devotional time with God.

A good modern Bible translation, such as the New International Version, the New American Standard Bible, or the New Revised Standard Version, will give you the most help in your study. You might also consider keeping a Bible dictionary handy to look up unfamiliar words, names, or places. Write your responses in the spaces provided in the study guide or use your personal journal if

What is Being Spiritual?

you need more space. This will help you participate more fully in the discussion, and will also help you personalize what you are learning.

When your group meets, be willing to join in the discussion. The leader of the group will not be lecturing but will encourage - people to discuss what they have learned from the study and exercise. Plan to share what God has taught you. Try to be sensitive to the other members of the group. Listen attentively when they speak, and be affirming whenever you can. This will encourage more hesitant members of the group to participate. Be careful not to dominate the discussion. By all means participate, but allow others to have equal time. If you are a group leader or a participant who wants further insights, you will find additional comments in the Leader's Guide at the back of the study.

We believe that your ongoing journey through this material will place you on an exciting path of spiritual adventure. Through your individual study time and group discussions, we trust you will enter into a fresh concept of spiritual life that will delight the heart of God . . . and your heart too!

Ten Core Values
for Spiritual Formation

Spiritual transformation . . .

   . . . is essential, not optional, for Christ-followers.

   . . . is a process, not an event.

   . . . is God's work, but requires my participation.

   . . . involves those practices, experiences, and relationships that help me live intimately with Christ and walk as if he were in my place.

   . . . is not a compartmentalized pursuit. God is not interested in my spiritual life; he's interested in my *life*—all of it.

   . . . can happen in every moment. It is not restricted to certain times or practices.

   . . . is not individualistic, but takes place in community and finds expression in serving others.

   . . . is not impeded by a person's background, temperament, life situation, or season of life. It is available right now to all who desire it.

   . . . and the means of pursuing it, will vary from one individual to another. Fully devoted followers are handcrafted, not mass-produced.

   . . . is ultimately gauged by an increased capacity to love God and people. Superficial or external checklists cannot measure it.

Growth: Training vs. Trying

S everal years ago, a group of teenage superheroes called the Mighty Morphin Power Rangers dominated the interest of most six year olds in the U.S. The show was an unlikely hit—originally produced on a very low budget in Japan, then badly dubbed into English. The key to the show's appeal was the characters' ability to "morph." With the rallying cry, "It's morphin' time!" normal adolescents were miraculously transformed into martial arts heroes for justice. The show became such a huge hit that the term *morph* began creeping into magazine articles and everyday conversations.

Does the word *morph* sound vaguely familiar? It is a part of *metamorphosis,* a word about transformation. The little word *morph* actually comes from one of the richest Greek words in the New Testament—*morphoo*—which means "the inward and real formation of the essential nature of a person." It was the term used to describe the formation and growth of an embryo in a mother's body. Paul used this word in his letter to the Galatians: " . . . until Christ is *formed* in you" (Gal. 4:19). Another form of the word appears when Paul says, "we, who with unveiled faces all reflect the Lord's glory, are being *transformed* into his likeness" (2 Cor. 3:18).

It's not just six year olds who want to morph. The desire for transformation is deep in the heart of every human.

The goal of spiritual transformation is to live as if Jesus held unhindered sway over your body. Of course, it is still *you* doing the living—your temperament, your gene pool, your history. But to grow spiritually means to increasingly live as Jesus would in your unique place—to see what Jesus would see if he looked through your eyes, to think what he would think, to feel what he would feel, and, therefore, to do what he would do.

Over time, an amazing thing can happen. You find yourself beginning to *want* to live this way. It appeals to you. It makes sense.

You no longer want to simply "do right things"; instead, you want to become the right kind of person.

Transformation is a holy and mysterious process. It doesn't happen quickly, neatly, or predictably. But the promise of Scripture is that ordinary people can receive power for extraordinary change.

It's morphing time!

Training to Live Like Jesus

Reading adapted from a message by John Ortberg

I vividly recall my first time on the Camp Paradise ropes course. (If you've never been on a ropes course, it's basically a high-wire experience for dummies, designed to stretch your abilities and help you overcome fear.) Allegedly, the ropes were thirty feet high, but I'm sure someone made a mistake. Clearly, I was thousands of feet in the air. Butterflies in attack formation assaulted my stomach. My sweat glands kicked into high gear. I was filled with anxiety. "This is not Camp Paradise," I thought. "This is Camp Purgatory. This is where they make you go to pay for your sins!"

The instructors moved across the ropes effortlessly and without fear. They had taught me that, because of the equipment and rope thickness, I was perfectly safe. Did I believe them? Part of me did. But not my stomach and sweat glands. I tried hard to stop my anxiety. I made every effort to feel and act as relaxed as my instructors did. But neither their teaching nor my willpower was enough to transform my inner being. There was only one way: I had to go through training. I had to *experience* the ropes course.

As I did, a change took place. Slowly, I came to trust that I really was safe. After a while, my whole being—even my stomach and sweat glands—began to believe it. I was being progressively transformed from a state of anxiety to a state of relaxed enjoyment. Training—practicing the ropes course day after day like the instructors did—allowed me to act with their same relaxed effortlessness.

Neither their teaching nor my willpower was enough to transform my inner being. There was only one way: I had to go through training.

Training vs. Trying

What does it mean to enter training? *It means to arrange your life around certain exercises and experiences that will enable you to do eventually what you are not yet able to do even by trying hard.* Training is essential for almost any significant endeavor in life — running a marathon, becoming a surgeon, learning how to play the piano. The need for preparation or training does not stop when it comes to learning the art of forgiveness, joy, or courage. It applies to a vibrant spiritual life just as it does to other activities. Learning to think, feel, and act like Jesus is at least as demanding as learning to run a marathon or play the piano.

To follow Jesus means learning to arrange my life around those practices that will enable me to stay connected to him and live more and more like him. In short, this is just another way of defining a spiritual discipline. *A spiritual discipline is any activity that can help me gain power to live life as Jesus taught and modeled it.*

What the Spiritual Disciplines Are *Not*

Unfortunately, for many people, the very concept of spiritual disciplines has become grossly distorted. So let's be clear about a few things.

Spiritual disciplines are not a barometer of spirituality. The ultimate indicator of your spiritual health is your capacity to fully love God and love people. If you can increase your capacity without the practice of any particular disciplines, then by all means skip them. Disciplines are never ends in themselves — only means to a greater end.

Spiritual disciplines are not a way to earn "brownie points" with God. They are not about meriting his forgiveness and goodwill. They are not "extra credit." They have value only insofar as they keep us vitally connected with Christ and empowered to live as he lived.

Similarly, a disciplined person is not necessarily someone who does a lot of disciplines. It is not a highly sys-

A spiritual discipine is any activity that can help me gain power to live life as Jesus taught and modeled it.

tematic, rigidly scheduled, chart-making, gold-star-loving early riser. *A disciplined person is one who can do the right thing at the right time in the right way with the right spirit.* A disciplined person is one who discerns when laughter, or gentleness, or silence, or healing words, or truth-telling is called for and offers it promptly, effectively, and in love.

Every Moment Counts

A group of us were discussing how to pursue spiritual life when one person, a mother with two young children, commented that it was easier for her to work on her spiritual life before she became a mom.

She had never been taught to consider the possibility that caring for two young children—carried out daily with expressions of gratitude, with prayers for help, and with patient acceptance of trials—might be a kind of "school of transformation" the likes of which she had never known before. To her, having a quiet time counted toward spiritual devotion, but caring for two children did not.

It all counts. Life counts. Every moment of life—at least potentially—is an opportunity to be guided by God into his way of living. Certainly, there are some foundational practices, like prayer, solitude, and Scripture meditation that are critically important. But all of life's activities can become spiritual training exercises if you allow them to.

Sitting in traffic congestion can become a training exercise in patience. Mundane activities like cleaning the house or taking a shower can train our hearts in gratitude, if we use those opportunities to thank God for his daily provisions. Delighting in nature or in wholesome pleasures can train our hearts in joy. Even sleep can be a spiritual discipline. Yes, you read that right! Disciplining ourselves to get a good night's sleep can train us away from anxiety and toward trust if we remind ourselves that the world is in God's hands and it will get along very well even though we're not awake to control everything.

A disciplined person is one who can do the right thing at the right time in the right way with the right spirit.

There is no need to divide life into times to "be spiritual" and times to "just do life." Every moment is a chance to learn from Jesus how to live in the kingdom of God.

God's Role and Mine

You may be wondering, "What about *God's* role in spiritual growth?" To speak of spiritual growth only as the product of training could make it sound like something that can be engineered.

Think of the difference between piloting a motorboat and a sailboat. I can run a motorboat all by myself. All I have to do is start the engine. I am in control. But a sailboat is a different story. I can hoist the sails. I can steer with the rudder. But I am utterly dependent on the wind. My job is simply to do those things that will enable me to catch the wind when it comes.

My job is to creatively and wisely engage in those activities that will give God a chance to work in my life.

Spiritual transformation is like piloting a sailboat. I can open myself to it through certain practices, but I cannot engineer the wind. When it comes, it is a kind of gift. Seeing this saves me from pride and from the wrong kind of effort. Wise sailors know their main task is to be able to read the wind, to learn to raise and lower particular sails to catch the wind most effectively. They know when to stay on the existing course and when to set a new one.

So it is with the spiritual disciplines. Our job is to creatively and wisely engage in those activities that will give God a chance to work in our life. This can look different in different seasons of our lives. We can put up the sails and adjust them as needed. But what happens is up to God.

"Follow Me"

Jesus came with the gracious announcement that it is possible to be changed. It is possible to live in such a way that people see you and say, "Wow! I didn't know that a life could look like that."

Do you believe this is really true, or might be true, or at least that you want it to be true? Then hear Jesus' invitation to you: "Follow me."

SPIRITUAL EXERCISE

Your challenge this week is to see that all of life counts. If you let them, the ordinary moments of your day can become powerful training exercises in spiritual transformation.

For one week, punctuate your days with the simple question, "How can *this moment* train me?" For example:

- You're in the "under ten items" checkout line behind someone who is either rude or mathematically challenged, and you're getting really frustrated. Stop and ask, "How can I use *this moment* to train me in patience and graciousness?"
- Someone offends you with a hurtful comment. You are just on the edge of hurting them back with a cutting remark. Stop and ask, "How can *this moment* train me in self-control and loving honesty?"
- You're on the verge of procrastinating (again) with a project you dislike. Stop and ask, "How can I respond in *this moment* in a way that will help train me in perseverance and faithfulness?"
- You're grumbling through daily chores—laundry, shopping, housecleaning, tasks at work. Stop in the midst and ask yourself, "How can I use *this moment* to train myself in gratitude for all that God's given me?"
- In the middle of a pressured day you encounter someone in need. Stop and ask yourself, "Might God want to use *this moment* to train me in kindness ... and to trust that I can be helpful and still accomplish what I need to?"

Again, these are just examples. The key is to bring this question to mind throughout the unique events of *your* day. On some days, you may know that you will be facing a difficult, tempting, or stretching situation. Consider praying a "how can *this moment* train me" prayer in advance.

Throughout the week, keep track of how this experience goes. How easy was it for you to stop yourself midstream? When did you feel like you got it right? How about times when your attempts failed? Do you notice any patterns to those experiences?

BIBLE STUDY

I magine that you knew you only had hours left to live. You would more than likely try to have one final conversation with the people closest to you. What would you say? What would your final words be? You would probably move quickly beyond small talk to those things of greatest importance to you; things you wanted your loved ones to hear and really *get;* things you wanted them to hold in their hearts forever. This is the context of Jesus' words in John chapters 14 and 15 as he prepares his disciples for his departure.

1. Jesus set high expectations for his followers. In John 14:12, he challenges them to live like him, doing the works that he did. What startling thing does Jesus go on to say in the last half of verse 12?

2. You would think that living this kind of life would require many things. But Jesus distills it to one thing required above all else. What is that one thing? (John 15:1 – 10)

3. Considering Jesus' illustration of a vine and a branch, put in your own words what it means to *abide* or *remain* in him.

4. How easily does abiding come for you? To what extent does your life naturally lend itself to abiding (remaining) in Christ?

Reflecting specifically on this past week, at what moment *did* you feel strongly connected to God—when abiding was a reality?

What factors contributed to that?

If you did not feel very connected to Christ, what were the obstacles?

5. Think back to this statement from the reading: "Training . . . means to arrange your life around those exercises and experiences that will enable you to do eventually what you are not yet able to do even by trying hard." What is the connection between training and abiding (or remaining) in Christ?

How do the words of Paul in 1 Corinthians 9:24–27 underscore the reality that learning to abide is not something into which we passively fall?

6. Return to Jesus' words in John 15:1–10. If we *are* living connected to Christ, something will be inevitable; if we are *not,* that same thing will be impossible. What is that thing? (See also verse 16.)

What sobering words does Jesus speak concerning those who consistently fail to bear good fruit?

NOTE: Jesus is clear: Living a fruitful life is not optional for believers. Fruitfulness is normal. So how do you know if you are really bearing the right kind of fruit?

It is critically important that we get clarity on this point. Being busy with a lot of Christian activities is not necessarily an indicator of fruitfulness. Neither is mastering the Bible or accumulating impressive spiritual accomplishments. The Pharisees did all these things and Christ declared them the least fruitful of all!

Jesus lived his life as a reflection of his Father. To see Jesus was to see God. To know one was literally to know the other (John 14:7−9). This is the ultimate test of our fruitfulness. When people see you, do they see Jesus? As they come to know you better, do they know him better? Paul goes one more step in unpacking this: "But the fruit of the Spirit is love, joy, peace, patience, kindness, goodness, faithfulness, gentleness and self-control" (Gal. 5:22−23).

7. Let's get practical. Reflect on your life and your patterns of relating during the past week. To what degree could it be said that to know you was to know Jesus with respect to these qualities?

	Low				High
LOVE	1	2	3	4	5

How tender was your heart toward God this week? Toward family and friends? Toward needy people? How did you reflect Jesus' love for lost people? Did you find yourself engaging in more acts of servanthood this week, or fewer? How often did a critical, judgmental spirit rear its head?

	Low				High
JOY	1	2	3	4	5

What was your irritability factor last week? Were you more inclined to speak words of complaint or words of gratitude? How often did you laugh? Did you have any fun? To what degree were you able to choose joy even during a time of frustration or difficulty? Do you find yourself even now rationalizing your lack of joy?

	Low				High
PEACE	1	2	3	4	5

To what degree was your heart and mind at rest in God last week? How consistently were you troubled and anxious? Was it a week of contentment or discontentment? Did you find yourself relating to others in a way that promoted peace, or did you stir up needless conflict?

	Low				High
PATIENCE	1	2	3	4	5

How did you respond when you didn't get your way or when you were frustrated? Were you able to wait gracefully when you needed to? How tolerant were you when someone wasn't performing as quickly as you wanted them to? (If you're already moving on to the next question, give yourself a 1 here!)

	Low				High
KINDNESS	1	2	3	4	5

How inclined were you to lend a helping hand even when you were busy? When you knew you wouldn't be recognized at all? Did you encourage or affirm anyone? How often did you say please and thank you? Were there times when your prejudices caused you to act unkindly to someone?

	Low				High
GENEROSITY	1	2	3	4	5

What portion of your time and material resources did you give to the work of God, to the poor, to others? Did you tend to give the least amount acceptable? Do you feel your heart growing or shrinking in this regard? Is your prevailing feeling that you never have quite enough or that you always have more than enough?

	Low				High
FAITHFULNESS	1	2	3	4	5

Would people around you say that you were dependable last week? How well did you keep your word, even with small things? How did you do with procrastination? How faithfully did you serve God by using your spiritual gifts last week? How obedient to God's Word were you?

	Low				High
GENTLENESS	1	2	3	4	5

How consistent were you in speaking truth with *grace*? How often did you get angry and inflict pain on someone? Are you growing in your ability to listen? Did you come alongside someone who was hurting to extend comfort? Were you moving too fast all week to even *think* of being gentle?

	Low				High
SELF-CONTROL	1	2	3	4	5

Were your bad habits more or less troubling to you last week? How likely were you to give in to damaging impulses? What about your mouth? How often did you speak without thinking? How inclined were you to say things (maybe in anger or maybe just to draw attention to yourself) that you knew should never have been said?

8. In what ways do you feel the affirmation of God that you really are growing and increasingly bearing good fruit?

What specific areas most need transforming? Honestly acknowledge those to God.

9. As you continue through this study, invite God to do his transforming work in your life. Ask him to show you how to creatively engage in the kind of spiritual training that will help you abide in him and bear much fruit.

TAKE-AWAY

My summary of the main point of this session, and how it impacts me personally:

NOTE: You will fill in this information after your small group discussion. Leave it blank until the conclusion of your meeting.

In next week's session, the spiritual exercise follows the Bible study. Please allow yourself enough time to complete the study early enough to concentrate on the exercise.

SESSION
TWO

The Practice of Scripture Meditation

Reading adapted from a message by John Ortberg

I f there is one thing we are serious about in our society, it's purity—at least when it comes to what we eat. The FDA establishes standards for everything sold in the market. Unfortunately, the standards of purity aren't always what you might hope.

Purity is a word greatly prized in the New Testament. Unfortunately, in our day it has been largely written off as quaint, Victorian, prudish.

Did you know that apple butter won't be sold if it has 5 or more whole insects per 100 grams? Otherwise it will go right onto your English muffins. Mushrooms can't be sold if there is an average of 20 or more maggots of any size per 15 grams of dried mushrooms. If there are more than 13 insect heads in 100 grams of fig paste, the FDA ruthlessly tosses the whole batch. As for hot dogs . . . it's best not to ask!

If anything is really good, we long for it to exist in its pure form. Oxygen without exhaust fumes. Snow unmixed with slush. When something is pure it exists in its undefiled, uncontaminated state.

Purity is a word greatly prized in the New Testament. Unfortunately, in our day it has been largely written off as quaint, Victorian, prudish. It sounds like a person who isn't fully human, when in fact God's call for us to be *pure* is precisely his call for us to be *purely human*—humanity as he intended it to be, uncontaminated by sin.

James calls the opposite of this condition being "double-minded" (James 4:8). He describes such a person as being like "a wave of the sea," driven forward by the wind one minute and backwards the next (James 1:6). It is a life of divided loyalties.

Most of us know what it is like to be a wave on the sea. We are pulled toward this life of Christ, and yet held back by a secret sin for which we haven't been willing to renounce or get help. We long for the adventure of following Christ fully, but we're afraid of the price. We commit to pleasing God alone, only to find ourselves driven to impress others. We go back and forth. It is a miserable way to live.

In Jesus' words, the secret to life is to pursue *one thing*. It is to seek first the kingdom of God and his righteousness (Matt. 6:33). It is an unbelievable relief to be delivered from double-mindedness, to finally decide, to stop being torn.

The secret to life is to pursue one thing. *It is to seek first the kingdom of God and his righteousness.*

Washed by the Word

If we want to be saved from double-mindedness and pursue purity of heart, we must "be transformed by the renewing of [our] mind" (Rom. 12:2). An indispensable practice is to have our minds re-formed by immersing them in Scripture. When Paul wrote to the church at Ephesus, he used this analogy: "Christ loved the church and gave himself up for her to make her holy, cleansing her by the washing with water through the word, and to present her to himself as a radiant church, without stain or wrinkle or any other blemish . . ." (Eph. 5:25–27).

We—the new community, the bride—are to be washed by the Word. Think of what happens when something gets washed. Soap and water move through the fibers of the dirty fabric at the deepest level, lifting out impurities and removing them from the fabric. Only after the washing can we see the fabric in the state for which it was originally designed.

So how do we read the Bible in a way that will wash our hearts and help us live like Jesus? Here are a few thoughts.

Ask God to Meet You in the Scriptures

It is uniquely in the Bible that we encounter Jesus. So before you begin to read, acknowledge that Jesus is present with you. Ask him to begin to wash your mind and thoughts—even if it stings a bit.

Meditate on a Fairly Brief Passage

It is important, of course, to be familiar with all of the Bible. Sometimes you will need to read broadly, but in reading for transformation you will need to go slowly. You can't meditate quickly. There is no Evelyn Woods course in speed-meditation.

Some time ago, I set a goal of praying through the Psalms, one psalm a day. Each day that I could check one off the list, I was one step closer to the goal. This meant I never wanted to get stuck on one psalm for two days in a row. It was as if God had a big chart on the refrigerator in heaven, and each time I made it through a psalm, I got a gold star. Naturally, this sabotaged God's real purpose. He wanted to speak to me, to renew me. What I had failed to realize was that if God is using one psalm, or even one word to do so, my job is to stick with it as long as it takes until I've learned what I need to learn. Your goal should not be for you to get through the Scriptures. The goal is to get the Scriptures through you.

The goal is not for you to get through the Scriptures. The goal is to get the Scriptures through you.

Read with a Readiness to Surrender

Don't read the Bible merely to find information, to increase your knowledge, or to be able to prove a point. Resolve that you will be obedient to it. Open your spirit and seek the Word's cleansing work.

One Sunday at my former church, I was verbally accosted by a man who was greatly admired for his knowledge of the Bible. He more or less appointed himself the watchdog for the church's doctrinal purity. It was a matter of deep importance to him that people know how well he knew the Scriptures. In a critical tone, he began to ruthlessly recite to me a litany of complaints about the church and my ministry. When he was done he said, "Remember, I don't like a lot of what you do, but I love you in the Lord."

I began to reflect on the little phrase—to love someone "in the Lord." Loving someone "in the Lord" means to love that person as the Lord himself would love him or her if in my place. Loving me "in the Lord" is precisely what this man didn't do. And the sad truth is, I didn't love him either. I didn't wish the best for him. I wanted to hear bad things about him. And the even more humbling truth is that the main reason I didn't love him was simply that he didn't like me. *I* needed to be washed.

To be filled with knowledge about the Bible but to be unwashed by it can be worse than not knowing at all.

Take One Thought or Verse with You throughout the Day

The psalmist says that fruitful living comes to the one who meditates on the law "day and night" (Psalms 1). Meditation is not meant to be spooky; it simply involves sustained attention. It is built on the principle that what the mind repeats, it retains.

If the Bible were to completely fulfill its mission in our lives, we would be transformed.

For one day, choose a single piece of Scripture—one "thought" of God's—to live with. Take, for instance, this thought from Psalm 46:10: "Be still, and know that I am God." For one day, live with those words. Commit them to memory. Let your mind continually return to them. Let them shape the way you do life that day. "Today—as best I can—I'm going to be still. I'm not going to chatter thoughtlessly. I will remember I don't have to defend myself or make sure people think of me the way I want them to. Today, I don't have to get my way. Before I make decisions I will try to listen for God's voice" . . . and so on.

As you do this, a wonderful thing will happen. You will discover that you really do *want* to be still. It really works better to let him be God instead of you.

If the Bible were to completely fulfill its mission in our lives, we would be transformed. We would be filled with thoughts and feelings of truth, love, joy, and humility. Every moment would be a miniature reflection of life in the kingdom of God. We need the practice of meditating on the Scriptures. We need to be washed. We need to be purely human.

BIBLE STUDY

NOTE: For this session, the spiritual exercise follows the Bible study. In order to try the spiritual experiment for the week, you will need to complete this study first. Don't wait until the last minute to prepare, or you won't have time to engage in the spiritual exercise before the meeting.

In this study, you will spend some time working through one method of biblical meditation called "Praying the Scriptures." The goal is to help you *metabolize*—take in and digest—God's truth as it is found in the Bible.

Let's use a familiar passage: Matthew 6:9–13, which contains "The Lord's Prayer." Before praying through it, answer the following questions to help you get a better background of the passage.

1. In the context where Jesus teaches this prayer, he expressly forbids two practices common to some people who thought they were praying correctly. What are those two praying errors mentioned in Matthew 6:5 and 7?

Jesus gives us clues to what is going on in these people's hearts when they pray in this unworthy fashion. What is the wrong attitude underlying these prayer mistakes?

2. To correct this warped understanding and practice of prayer, Jesus offers a new pattern for praying. He chooses to begin with the words, "Our Father in heaven . . ." Why do you think he began that way? (See Rom. 8:15–16; Eph. 2:19; Matt. 7:7–11)

NOTE: By proposing we address God as "Father," Jesus was making a break with the Judaism of his day that had many reverent names for God, but no common practice of calling him "Father." It's hard to overestimate the impact this new convention would have had among devout Jews unaccustomed to such familial designations. Abraham, Isaac, Jacob—these great men were "the fathers." But God? Clearly, Jesus wanted his followers to know of God's closeness and personal availability when they pray.

This is further underscored by Jesus asking us to call God our Father "in heaven." Heaven is not a faraway place. It is the dwelling of God; but God is, of course, omnipresent—no point anywhere is distant from him, including the point where you are at this moment. God is called "heavenly Father" because everything true of heaven—its goodness, its purity, its splendor—are all true of God. He is better than the best earthly father to an infinite degree. When God answers our prayers, heaven comes on earth in a limited way, showing how close heaven and our heavenly Father really are.

3. Consider what it means to "hallow" God's name. The meaning of the word *holy* is literally to be "set apart; different." To hallow something is to recognize its intrinsic specialness.

Why would Jesus want us to focus on God's holiness early in each prayer?

4. How would your prayers be different if you believed God was a tender Father, but *not* a perfect and powerful God? Or that he was perfect and powerful but *not* a tender Father?

Do you tend to pray with one orientation more than the other?

What is the impact of Jesus combining *both* aspects of who God is?

5. What do you think Jesus is saying when he asks for God's kingdom to come? What clarification is brought by the phrase that follows in the same verse?

NOTE: In praying "your kingdom come," Jesus is not just praying about a future event. Certainly, the day is coming when Jesus will return and establish his kingdom in all its fullness. But that does not mean we are simply treading water waiting for a future happening. Each time I sincerely seek to do God's will, his kingdom breaks into the world in and through me. God's kingdom is present right here and now, and each moment is a chance to live in it and pray for its spreading.

6. When the children of Israel followed Moses into the wilderness, they were given a form of daily bread called manna. Read Exodus 16:11–21. Do you see any connections between the experience of Israel and Jesus telling us to pray for daily bread?

What spiritual lesson do you think God was trying to teach Israel at that time?

What might be an application of that lesson for us today?

What further truth about daily bread does Jesus teach us in John 6:32–35?

7. Jesus goes on to pray for God to forgive us as we forgive others. Consider these two statements:

Our hands are not open to receive mercy when they are clenched tightly around resentments.

Our hands cannot clench tightly around resentment when they are filled with mercy.

What is the inevitable two-way connection between experiencing God's forgiving grace and extending forgiving grace to others? (See Matt. 18:23–35)

8. By including a reference to the evil one in Jesus' model prayer, of what reality about the spiritual world do you think Jesus wants us to be mindful? Why?

NOTE: The phrase "For thine is the kingdom, and the power, and the glory, forever. Amen." is familiar to many of us from the King James translation or from the song derived from it. It is a wonderfully worshipful ending to the prayer. It is not, however, in the earliest and most reliable manuscripts, so recent translations like the New International Version or the New Revised Standard Version do not include it as part of the oldest biblical text.

Now, let's move strictly into meditation on the Word and praying through the passage. Read through Matthew 6:9–13 once more in its entirety. Then take a phrase at a time. Reflect on its meaning, mull it over, digest it. Specifically, how does the truth you are reading relate to *you* right now in your setting? Then, talk to God based on those thoughts. Here is an example:

"Our Father in heaven . . ."

Spend some time reflecting on the intimacy God wants with *you*—that of all the names that are rightfully his, he wants you to call him Father. What's the implication of that truth? What feelings does it stir? How would your life today be different if you really related to him in that way? . . . *Lord, sometimes I still have a hard time believing that I can call you Father. Thank you that I don't need to be afraid of you. You tell me that I have a privileged position in you. I really want to experience your fatherly love more deeply; I know I would live with more confidence and freedom if I did. Help me to break down the barriers. . . .*

Continue line by line through the passage, using the phrases as "triggers" to generate your own reflections, requests, and expressions of worship. Be attentive to feelings that may well up along the way; invite God to be a part of them, too. The point is to personalize the passage, keeping the truth of Scripture intact.

Some people find they focus best if they write out their thoughts as they are flowing—others do not. Do what feels best for you. If questions come up, bracket them for later study rather than getting bogged down trying to find an immediate answer.

Remember, you can't meditate fast. Go slowly. If God is using one phrase—or even one word—to do a good work in you, stick with it. It may take several days or even more to work through the passage. Again, the goal is not to get through the Scriptures, but to get the Scriptures through *you*.

When you're done, think back over the experience. What happened to you as you reflected and prayed? When was it difficult? When did it seem to flow? Was there a particular truth God seemed to be trying to impress upon you? How did you respond?

SPIRITUAL EXERCISE

Now that you've completed the study and meditation, choose one phrase to take with you through the week. Was there a phrase that was especially meaningful? One that God really used to wash you or to strengthen you?

For example, you might carry with you the small phrase "Your kingdom come." Consider how you would act if Jesus were in your place by applying that simple concept throughout the day. Observe your actions, your relating patterns, by asking, "How is this manifesting your kingdom, God?" Look for hidden places in your heart where you feel resistance. Become aware of those times when your focus shifts back to making your *own* kingdom come. By continually reminding yourself of the little phrase "Your kingdom come," see how much easier it is to have Jesus' mind and strength throughout your day.

Write down the phrase you will take with you this week:

TAKE-AWAY

My summary of the main point of this session, and how it impacts me personally:

> NOTE: You will fill in this information after your group discussion. Leave it blank until the conclusion of your meeting.

SESSION
THREE

THE PRACTICE
OF SOLITUDE

The Practice of Solitude

Reading adapted from a message by John Ortberg

Not long after moving to Chicago, I called a wise friend to ask for some spiritual direction. I described the pace at which things tend to move in my setting. I told him of the rhythms of our family life, about the present condition of my heart as best I could discern it. What did I need to do, I asked him, to be spiritually healthy?

There was a long pause. "You must ruthlessly eliminate hurry from your life," he said slowly. Another long pause.

"Okay, I've written that one down," I told him, a little impatiently. "Now what else is there?" I had many things to do and this was a long-distance call, so I was anxious to cram as many units of spiritual wisdom into the least amount of time possible.

"There is nothing else," he said.

This is the wisest spiritual mentor I have ever known. He knows me well. And from an immense quiver of spiritual wisdom he drew only one arrow. "You must ruthlessly eliminate hurry from your life."

Suffering from Hurry Sickness

We suffer from what has come to be known as hurry sickness. We worship at the shrine of the Golden Arches not because they sell good food or even cheap food but *fast* food. And even after the invention of fast food, people still had to take the time to park their cars and go inside to

"You must ruthlessly eliminate hurry from your life."

order and eat—which took time. So we invented the drive-thru lane. Now families can eat in vans, as God intended.

Take this little test. Do you find yourself reading faster, talking faster, and when listening, nodding faster to try to get the speaker to accelerate? At a stoplight, if there are two lanes each containing one car, do you find yourself guessing—based on the year, make, and model of each car—which one will pull away the fastest?

If so, there's a good chance you've got hurry sickness.

Hurry is the great enemy of spiritual life in our day. For most of us, the danger is not that we will renounce our faith. It is that we will become so distracted and rushed and preoccupied that we will settle for a mediocre version of it. Hurry will destroy your soul. It will keep you from life. Depth always comes slowly; this is simply a truth about human formation. You cannot microwave maturity.

Perhaps the most serious aspect of hurry sickness is a damaged capacity to love.

Perhaps the most serious aspect of hurry sickness is a damaged capacity to love. For love and hurry are fundamentally incompatible. Love always takes time. Hurry kills love. Hurry prevents us from receiving love from the Father or giving it to his children.

In the final analysis, hurry is not just a disordered schedule. *Hurry is a disordered heart.*

But there is hope. You can change. You really can. But it will not happen merely by trying. Once again, you must enter a life of training.

Follow the Leader

At the beginning of his ministry, Jesus went to the wilderness for an extended period of fasting and prayer. He also withdrew when he heard of the death of John the Baptist, again when he was choosing his disciples, and frequently after a full day of ministry. The practice continued through his final days, when he withdrew to a garden to pray. He ended his ministry as he began it, with the practice of solitude.

Jesus was often busy, but never hurried. He had much to do, but he never did it in a way that severed the life-giving connection between himself and his Father. He never did it in a way that interfered with his ability to give love. He observed a regular rhythm of withdrawal from activity for solitude and prayer.

And he taught his followers to do the same: "Come with me by yourselves to a quiet place and get some rest," he said to them (Mark 6:31)—and he says to them still. Following Jesus cannot be done at a sprint. If you want to follow someone, *you can't go faster than the one who is leading.*

Solitude

Wise followers of Jesus have always understood solitude to be a foundational practice—the furnace of transformation. But what exactly is solitude? People wonder sometimes: What do I do when I practice solitude? What should I bring with me?

At its heart, solitude is primarily about not *doing something.*

The primary answer, of course, is *nothing.* Not long ago, a man told how he prepared for his first extended period of solitude: He brought along books, tapes, CDs, and a VCR—the very things you go into solitude to get away *from.*

At its heart, solitude is primarily about *not* doing something. When I go into solitude, I withdraw from conversation, from the presence of others, from noise, from the constant barrage of stimulation. I leave behind all the stuff I use to keep myself propped up. I have no friends to talk with, no phone calls, no TV to entertain, no pile of books to occupy or distract. I am, in the words of the old hymn, "just as I am"—not my accomplishments, my possessions, or my relationships. Just me and my sinfulness; my desire for God and my lack of desire for God.

Of course, solitude may be used as an occasion to engage in other practices as well. Prayer, self-examination, and meditation on Scripture are probably the most helpful practices to engage in during solitude.

I find it helpful to think about solitude in two categories. I need brief periods on a regular basis—preferably each day. Sometimes I begin the day by praying over the day's schedule. I anticipate tasks I must perform, people I will be with, meetings I will be in, and place it all in God's hands, asking for his strength and wisdom.

Throughout the day I may take five-minute breaks to reconnect with God and to remind myself of his presence. Sometimes in the evening, I review the day with God — to see what he might want to say to me and to hand any anxieties over to him.

Several times a year, I also need extended periods of solitude — a half day, a day, or a few days. Unless I pull out my calendar and block out times in advance, they will not happen. But they are critical times for more significant review of the work of God in my life.

Don't Give Up

Pursuing solitude will take relentless perseverance.

Pursuing solitude will take relentless perseverance. At first, you may even feel it's a waste of time. This is because we are conditioned to feel that our existence is justified only when we are doing something or accomplishing something.

You may feel frustrated at your inability to stay focused. The first time I tried extended solitude, my mind wandered like a tourist with a Eurail pass. I have come to realize, over time, that focused prayer, interspersed with wanderings, is all my mind is capable of now. In his book *The Practice of the Presence of God,* Brother Lawrence put it this way: "For many years, I was bothered by the thought that I was a failure at prayer. Then one day, I realized I would always be a failure at prayer; and I've gotten along much better ever since."

Are you tired of the effects of your hurry sickness? Don't you feel a yearning for something more? A pull toward a deeper, fuller experience of God's presence? If so, it's time to enter training for another way to live. The practice of solitude will begin opening that door.

SPIRITUAL EXERCISE

Your challenge this week is to "ruthlessly eliminate hurry from your life." We are not asking you to stop being busy. Rather, this exercise is designed to help you train yourself away from the kind of hurriedness that keeps you chronically preoccupied and anxious—that hinders you from receiving love from the Father and giving it to others. Here are a few exercises with which to experiment:

- Write out the words, "You cannot go faster than the One who is leading." Post this phrase on your mirror, your car visor, your desk. Take it with you throughout each day this week.
- Even before you get out of bed each morning, pause to acknowledge God's presence. Thank him for seeing you through the night. Invite him to be with you through the day. Enjoy the little solitude that those early morning moments present—even if they are only moments.
- As you eat your meals today, slow down. Chew your food deliberately. Really taste it. Enjoy it. Thank God for it. As you are driving, pick the slow lane at least a few times each day. Pray occasionally as you drive. Take advantage of the solitude that bumper-to-bumper traffic can provide.
- Resolve to take this day one activity at a time. Commit to being genuinely present in each moment. If your mind starts racing to the next thing, stop. Entrust it to God and return to the needs of the moment.
- Take a five-minute break once or twice in your day. Consciously reconnect with God. Ask yourself, "Am I going faster today than the One who is leading?"
- Listen—really listen—to the people with whom you have conversations today. Consider secretly saying a prayer for them as you speak. See if you can make it through an entire conversation without interrupting.
- Before going to bed, spend a few moments reflecting on the day—the times when you got it right and the times when you didn't. See what God might want to say to you. Hand your anxieties over to him. Rest in the promise of his grace.

BIBLE STUDY

1. Read 1 John 4:7–12, then consider the phrase from the reading, "hurry kills love." Reflecting on this past week, were there ways in which that proved true for you (either in receiving God's love or in extending it)?

> NOTE: There is an important distinction between being busy and being hurried. Being busy simply means that we have many things to do. It refers to the outward activities of our lives. People like Jesus and Paul were often busy. Being busy is not necessarily bad. Some of us are capable of living fairly fast-paced lives in ways that do not damage the health of our heart and spirit. True spirituality is not a nostalgic longing for a slower-paced, simpler world.
>
> Hurriedness is another story. It is a condition of the inner life, of the spirit. When we are hurried, we find ourselves preoccupied, anxious, easily irritated, unable to be fully present in the moment, joyless, unable to receive or give love.

2. Considering the above, indicate where your life falls on the following scale:

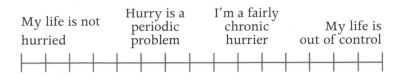

My life is not hurried   Hurry is a periodic problem   I'm a fairly chronic hurrier   My life is out of control

3. Ecclesiastes 5:1 admonishes, "Guard your steps when you go to the house of God. Go near to listen rather than to offer the sacrifice of fools...." How does frantic, noisy living cause your life to sometimes turn into "the sacrifice of a fool"?

We are usually surrounded by so much outer noise that it is hard to truly hear our God when he is speaking to us. We have often become deaf.... Thus our lives have become absurd. In the word absurd *we find the Latin word* surdus, *which means "deaf."* ...

When, however, we learn to listen, our lives become obedient lives. The word obedient *comes from the Latin word* audire, *which means "listening." A spiritual discipline is necessary in order to move slowly from an absurd to an obedient life, from a life filled with noisy worries to a life in which there is some free inner space where we can listen to our God and follow his guidance.*

—Henri Nouwen, *Making All Things New*

4. Read Luke 6:12–19. Notice that Jesus follows a three-step progression in this snapshot of a day in his life. Identify those three steps below:

v. 12

v. 13

vv. 17–19

NOTE: Henri Nouwen observed that we often get the order of events backward in our lives. We engage in ministry which leads to frustration so we ask some other people for help, which often creates further difficulties. When all else fails, we spend some time alone with God trying to rectify the mess. We follow the order of ministry, community, solitude rather than the other way around.

5. Why do you think there is a human tendency to start with activity rather than spending time alone with Christ?

6. How does the story recorded in Luke 10:38–42 reinforce that tendency?

What do you think explains Jesus' reaction to Martha?

Do you think Mary was lazy? Why was she commended?

In what ways are you sometimes like Martha?

7. Look at the following examples of Jesus in solitude. What need was solitude serving for Jesus at that time?

Mark 1:21−39

Luke 6:12−16

Mark 6:30−32

Matthew 14:6−13

Matthew 26:36−46

8. What work do you think God longs to do in your life that he probably will not be able to do until you become more intentional about practicing solitude?

TAKE-AWAY

My summary of the main point of this session, and how it impacts me personally:

NOTE: You will fill in this information after your group discussion. Leave it blank until the conclusion of your meeting.

Simple Prayer

Reading adapted from *Prayer: Finding the Heart's True Home*, by Richard J. Foster

We today yearn for prayer and hide from prayer. We are attracted to it and repelled by it. We believe prayer is something we should do, even something we want to do, but it seems like a chasm stands between us and actually praying. We know the agony of prayerlessness.

We assume that prayer is something to master the way we master algebra.

We are not quite sure what holds us back. Of course we are busy with work and family obligations, but that is only a smoke screen. No, there is something deeper, more profound keeping us in check. It is the notion—almost universal among us modern high achievers—that we have to have everything "just right" in order to pray. Our lives need some fine tuning, or we need to know more about how to pray, or we need to study the philosophical questions surrounding prayer. We assume that prayer is something to master the way we master algebra. We want to be competent and in control. But what we really need is to deliberately surrender control and become incompetent.

Just As We Are

I used to think that I needed to get all my motives straightened out before I could pray, really pray. I would be in some prayer group and I would examine what I had just prayed and think to myself, "How utterly foolish and self-centered; I can't pray this way!" And so I would determine never to pray again until my motives were pure. I didn't want to be a hypocrite. But the practical effect of all this internal soul-searching was to completely paralyze my ability to pray.

The truth of the matter is, we all come to prayer with a tangled mass of motives — good *and* selfish, merciful *and* hateful, loving *and* bitter. Frankly, this side of eternity we will *never* fully unravel the good from the bad, the pure from the impure. But what I have come to see is that God is big enough to receive us with all our mixture. We do not have to be bright, or pure, or filled with faith, or anything. That is what *grace* means, and not only are we saved by grace, we live by it as well. And we pray by it.

Simple Prayer

Not only are we saved by grace, we live by it as well. And we pray by it.

God receives us just as we are and accepts our prayers just as they are. In the same way that a small child cannot draw a bad picture, a child of God cannot offer a bad prayer. So we are brought to the most basic, the most primary, form of prayer: Simple Prayer.

Simple Prayer is found throughout Scripture. It involves ordinary people bringing ordinary concerns to a loving and compassionate Father. There is no pretense in Simple Prayer. We do not pretend to be more holy, more pure, or more saintly than we actually are. We do not try to conceal our conflicting and contradictory motives from God — or ourselves. In this posture we pour out our heart to the God who is greater than our heart and who knows all things (1 John 3:19–20).

Simple Prayer is beginning prayer. It is the prayer of children and yet we will return to it again and again. Jesus calls us to Simple Prayer when he urges us to ask for daily bread. We never outgrow this kind of prayer, because we never outgrow the needs which give rise to it.

There is a temptation, especially by the "sophisticated," to despise this most elementary way of praying. Grandly they speak of avoiding "self-centered prayer." What they fail to see, however, is that Simple Prayer is necessary, even essential, to the spiritual life. The only way we move beyond "self-centered prayer" (if indeed we ever do) is by going through it, not by making a detour around it. When we pray, genuinely pray, the real condition of our heart is revealed. This is as it should be. This is when God truly begins to work with us. The adventure is just beginning.

Beginning Where We Are

So how do we practice Simple Prayer? What do we do? Where do we begin?

We begin right where we are: in our families, on our jobs, with our neighbors and friends. I wish this did not sound so trivial, because on the practical level of knowing God it is the most profound truth we will ever hear. To believe that God can reach us and bless us in the ordinary junctures of daily life is the stuff of prayer. The only place God can bless us is right where we are, because that is the only place we are!

"Lay before Him what is in us, not what ought to be in us."

Perhaps we have a crushing failure that gives us more than one sleepless night. Well, we pace the floor *with* God, telling him of our hurt and our pain and our disappointment. We cry out, "why me?" for frustration and tears and anger are also the language of Simple Prayer. We invite God to walk with us as we grieve the loss of our dream. We speak frankly and honestly about what is happening and ask God to help us see the hurt behind the emotion.

God is perfectly capable of handling our anger, frustration, and disappointment. C. S. Lewis counsels us to "lay before Him what is in us, not what *ought* to be in us." God listens in compassion and love, just like we do when our children come to us. He delights in our presence. When we do this, we will discover something of inestimable value. We will discover that by praying we learn to pray.

A Few Words of Counsel

First, as we begin, we must never be discouraged by our lack of prayer. Even in our prayerlessness we can hunger for God. If so, the hunger itself is prayer—the prayer of desire. In time the desire will lead to practice, and the practice will increase the desire. When we cannot pray, we let God be our prayer. Nor should we be frightened by the hardness of our heart; prayer will soften it. We even give our lack of prayer to God.

An opposite but equally important counsel is to let go of trying *too* hard to pray. Some people work at the business of praying with such intensity that they get spiritual indigestion. There is a principle of progression in the spiritual life. We do not take occasional joggers and put them in a marathon. If prayer is not a fixed habit with you, instead of starting with hours of prayer, single out a few moments and put all your energy into them. When you have had enough, tell God simply, "I must have a rest."

Finally, we should learn to pray even while we are dwelling on evil. Perhaps we are waging an interior battle over anger, lust, pride, or greed. We need not isolate these things from prayer. Instead we talk to God about what is going on inside that we know displeases him. We lift our disobedience into the arms of the Father; he is strong enough to carry the weight. Sin may separate us from God, but trying to hide our sin separates us all the more. "The Lord," writes Emilie Griffin, "loves us—perhaps most of all—when we fail and try again."

"The Lord loves us—perhaps most of all—when we fail and try again."

The Conversion of the Heart

In the beginning we are indeed the subject and center of our prayers. But in God's time and in God's way a revolution takes place in our heart. Slowly, almost imperceptibly, there is a shift in our center of gravity. We pass from thinking of God as part of our life to the realization that we are part of *his* life. Mysteriously, God moves from the edges of our prayer experience to the center. A conversion of the heart takes place, a transformation of the spirit. It is a wonderful work of Divine Grace.

Excerpt adapted from *Prayer: Finding the Heart's True Home,* by Richard J. Foster. Copyright © 1992 by Richard J. Foster. Reprinted by permission of HarperCollins Publishers, Inc.

PURSUING SPIRITUAL TRANSFORMATION

Make today an experiment in Simple Prayer. Seek to keep a secret, inner conversation running with God throughout your day. Continually let him know what you are thinking, hoping, fearing, desiring. Don't try to sanitize these conversations or make them "sound" prayerful. Just share whatever is on your mind. When you discover that your mind has drifted, don't feel guilty. Simply bring your attention back to his presence.

- When you wake up, greet the Lord to begin your day. Invite him to be a part of all you do.
- When you feel joy through the day, offer thanks.
- Use anxiety as a cue for prayer. Don't try to stop worrying; simply express your concerns to God.
- Offer "flash prayers" for each person you meet. As you outwardly converse with people, inwardly pray for God's blessing on their lives.
- When you catch yourself dwelling on something evil—lust, greed, pride, etc.—don't isolate it from God. (He knows it anyway!) Talk to him about what you know is displeasing him.
- When you face problems or confusion, ask God for wisdom.
- When you feel frustration or disappointment, honestly communicate that to God. Don't censor your feelings.

Observe how this time goes. Was it easy or difficult to engage in this kind of prayer? Were there times when you thought, "I can't say *that* to God?" Were you able to talk to him even in the midst of a sinful moment? Did you notice anything different happening in your relationship with God as you prayed this way?

BIBLE STUDY

The first prayer in the Bible is found in Genesis 3:10. Although Adam and God certainly conversed on several occasions prior to this exchange, the first recorded words a human being says to God are found in this verse. They come immediately after Adam and Eve have disobeyed God and eaten the forbidden fruit.

1. Why did Adam say he was hiding?

What do you think is the real reason he avoided God?

What emotion was he feeling?

2. Read Psalm 32:1−4. What were the results of David's hiding?

3. What do you learn from these two examples about human tendencies in prayer when sin is present?

4. Consider again Richard Foster's words:

   There is no pretense in Simple Prayer. We do not pretend to be more holy, more pure, or more saintly than we actually are.

   How would your own prayer life be different if you *really* believed that?

5. In Genesis 18:22−33, Abraham has a frank conversation with God, who appeared in human form to him just before God destroyed Sodom and Gomorrah. Abraham's nephew Lot and his family lived in that city. What is the issue Abraham discusses with God?

   What is Abraham's tone during the conversation?

Does God appear upset with Abraham's questioning of him?

Do you think Abraham was being overly concerned with sounding nonargumentative?

6. Moses had a similarly candid "negotiation" with God recorded in Exodus 32. The Israelites had turned their back on God to worship the golden calf that they had crafted. God's anger burned, and he intended to destroy the entire nation (vv. 8–10).

How does Moses intervene (vv. 11–13)? What bold requests does he make to God?

How do you react to Moses' forcefulness?

How did God respond (v. 14)?

7. The Bible even includes prayers so honest that they have come to be known by some as "Prayers of Complaint." Also known as "Lament Psalms," most of them were written by David—"a man after God's own heart." Richard Foster makes this observation about these psalms:

They expressed reverence and disappointment ... dogged hope and mounting despair ... confidence in the character of God and exasperation at the inaction of God. ... The Lament Psalms teach us to pray our inner conflicts and contradictions.

—*Prayer: Finding the Heart's True Home*

Read through Psalm 13, an example of a Lament Psalm. Does it feel in any way inappropriate to you to address God this way? Why?

What about David's view of God keeps this kind of honesty from turning into chronic complaining — or even outright arrogance (see vv. 5 and 6)? What important things keep us rooted in humility even when we are praying with this level of honesty?

8. How did Jesus model simple, honest prayer during the last day of his life?

Matthew 26:36–46

Matthew 27:45–46

Luke 23:44–46

9. Read the following three hallmark verses on prayer. Rewrite their content in your own words, stating it as if God were speaking directly to you.

Hebrews 4:14−16

Philippians 4:6–7

1 Peter 5:7

TAKE-AWAY

My summary of the main point of this session, and how it impacts me personally:

NOTE: You will fill in this information after your group discussion. Leave it blank until the conclusion of your meeting.

In next week's lesson, the Bible study and spiritual exercise are combined into a single solitude experience. You will need to set aside a block of time for this experience.

SESSION
FIVE

THREE TRANSFORMING
PRAYERS

Three Transforming Prayers

Reading adapted from a message by Bill Hybels

You've probably seen the signs that say "Swim at Your Own Risk" or "Ski at Your Own Risk" or "Ride at Your Own Risk." I was at a cheap truck stop once and saw a sign that said, "Eat at Your Own Risk." Not a very encouraging sign!

I think there needs to be a sign, "Pray at Your Own Risk." Because there are certain kinds of prayers that can wreak all kinds of havoc in your life. They upset your applecart, they throw a wrench into your meticulously planned future, they take you down unexpected paths. They are risky prayers, but prayers we must begin to pray if we genuinely want to be transformed.

There are certain kinds of prayers that can wreak all kinds of havoc in your life.

Search Me

"Search me, O God, and know my heart; test me and know my anxious thoughts. See if there is any offensive way in me." Perhaps you've heard these words before, but maybe not in context. In Psalm 139, David was praying and he was filled with worship for his wonderful God. But as he's giving praise, something else happens in his mind. He begins picturing people who are rebellious to God — people whose lifestyles fly in the face of everything a holy God stands for. And so, in the middle of his worship, David cries out, "Do I not hate those who hate you, O LORD. . .? I have nothing but hatred for them" (vv. 21–22).

He's saying, "I just don't get it. How could any living being refuse to follow a God as wonderful as you?"

And in that moment—like lightning striking on a hot August night—the thought strikes him, "Wait! Here I am thinking about all those people out there that might not be fully submitted to God. Maybe there is a little pocket of rebellion or resistance in *me*. Maybe there is a dark little closet somewhere in my soul that is not fully yielded to God." And David can't bear the thought of that.

So, with extraordinary courage he says, "Search *me*, God. Test *me*. Expose whatever secret exists in *me* that is not fully surrendered. Bring it out into the light. Expose it so that by your power and grace it can be touched and removed and put out of my life, because I don't want anything in my life to be a deterrent to my full devotion to you."

What a prayer!

It's a lot easier to ask God to deal with other people than it is to get on your knees and say, "God, deal with me. Deal with me." Have you ever prayed that prayer? Are you willing to pray that prayer? It's a high-risk thing.

It's a lot easier to ask God to deal with other people than it is to get on your knees and say, "God, deal with me. Deal with me."

Perhaps you don't pray that "search me" prayer because you *know* where the Holy Spirit's spotlight would go. Perhaps it's a practice that nobody knows about that you've been engaging in. It dishonors God, it beats up your self-esteem, it drags you down spiritually—but it's hard to let some of these things go, isn't it? And the Holy Spirit is saying, "Let it go! You don't want to live the rest of your life with that hole in your boat. Let it go."

Perhaps, if you pray the "search me" prayer, the Spirit would tell you to get out of or redefine a relationship that has become an integrity issue in your life. Or the light might shine on the way you're treating your body, or how you're handling your money, what you're doing with your temper, or how you are nursing your grudges.

It's a prayer we all must pray if we're really serious about growing. And when we pray it, the Holy Spirit will answer. He will. He'll put the light on something, and it will get exposed. And at that moment you've got the big choice to make: Will you repent, will you trust, will you put it behind you, will you let it go?

Someday you'll look back over your shoulder and you'll say, "I'm so glad I prayed that prayer and that God answered it." But pray it at your own risk.

Stretch Me

In the first century when the first church was being built, the Romans and others were persecuting the Christians. Believers were being hunted down, beaten, often murdered for their faith.

In Acts 4, we read that the core believers in that early church got together and decided they needed to pray. What do you think they prayed? They prayed, in essence, "Lord, increase our courage and our faith. We don't want to cave in. We want to take a stand. We want to be bold . . . all the way to the end, if it goes that way. Stretch our faith!"

What a prayer! If I had been in that situation, I'd be praying, "God, send guns. Improve my aim. Get me out of this mess." Instead, they prayed, "Stretch us to meet the opposition!"

Have you ever prayed a "stretch me" prayer? They come in all kinds of flavors. For example, you're standing in a long line of people, steaming with intense frustration because the line isn't moving fast enough for you. Then a thought comes to your mind. Instead of praying, "Make this line go faster," you say, "Stretch me, God. Stretch my patience in this situation, increase my self-control, diminish my homicidal tendencies!"

Or perhaps you're moving fast in a very pressured day. But you come across someone in need. And you stop and pray a "stretch me" prayer. "Stretch my compassion, Lord. Stretch my faith to believe that I can express kindness right here in this moment and that my day will still be okay. I'll get my work done. Stretch my capacity to love."

Have you ever prayed a prayer like this? "Stretch my giving, God. Stretch my heart to be able to provide resources for this person without worrying whether or not you're going to resupply my resource bank."

Someday you'll look back over your shoulder and you'll say, "I'm so glad I prayed that prayer and that God answered it."

This is the "stretch me" prayer — to have a bigger heart, to have a deeper faith, to be bold and take a stand when everyone else is caving in. God will answer it. But you have to pray it.

Lead Me

This prayer gives us no relief from danger whatsoever. It should have a neon warning light attached to it. I know of few other prayers that can have as sweeping a set of consequences associated with it. "Lead me."

Your life is really important. It's the only one you have. The past is gone. You have only from this day until your last day to be on the adventure that God has in mind for you.

He leads in small ways. Throughout the day, if you're in a position to listen, he may prompt you to encourage someone, to mend a relationship, to carry out a specific act of servanthood. Sometimes he leads in larger ways that can alter the whole trajectory of your life.

In any case, God tends not to wrestle the controls of people's lives from their hands. Do you want to run your life? God will most likely say, "Go ahead." But he will also say, "I have a better path. I have one that will help your life count more. I have one that will more deeply satisfy your soul." God tends only to lead when he's invited to do so, which is why I urge you to get to a quiet place and get on your knees and say, "God, lead my life. I only have from here to the end. Lead it."

Search me. Stretch me. Lead me. Three high-risk prayers. Three prayers that have the power to transform your life.

You have only from this day until your last day to be on the adventure that God has in mind for you.

BIBLE STUDY
AND SPIRITUAL EXERCISE

This week, the Bible study and spiritual exercise are combined into a single solitude experience focused around the three prayers presented in the reading. Schedule a time—we suggest a few hours, minimally—when you will be fairly rested and alert. If it is not possible to set aside that amount of time, consider praying through these prayers in three separate sittings.

The objective is not necessarily getting through everything here in detail, but rather to connect with God and to hear him. This is designed so you can immerse yourself—lose yourself, so to speak—in an encounter with the living God. Through times like this, you enter his realm still present in this world, but aware of unseen realities as well. Therefore, it would be better to finish only one part of the exercise and have God do his work in you than to complete everything hurriedly without having a personal experience with God.

Find a place where you will be alone, free from distractions and interruptions. Make it a place where you can be comfortable. If possible, pick a setting pleasing to you. Bring a Bible, and a journal or pad of paper to record your thoughts.

The outline below will guide you through this time, but, by all means, follow the Holy Spirit as he prompts you. Again, the goal is not just to complete an assignment; the goal is to quiet yourself before God, review his work in your life, and hear the words he has just for you.

Still Yourself

One of the hardest things to do in our daily busyness is simply to *stop*. Being quiet usually produces boredom, anxiety, or drowsiness. But in order to embark on this exercise, you must deliberately be still. That means your body is still, your mind stops racing, your thoughts become directed instead of reactive. Don't trouble yourself with what you have to do later or what happened yesterday. You can think about all that later. If these thoughts pop up along the way, "park them" on your pad of paper so they don't interfere with your concentration.

Invite God's Presence

Acknowledge that God is present with you right now. Thank him for his never-failing companionship. Place yourself in his hands. Ask him to help you be sensitive to his leadings. Invite him to speak to you in whatever way is most needed as you engage in the following time of reflection and prayer.

Personal Review and Prayer

"Search Me" Prayer

Search me, O God, and know my heart; test me and know my anxious thoughts. See if there is any offensive way in me, and lead me in the way everlasting.

—Psalm 139:23–24

Begin by turning to Psalm 139. You will be using this psalm as a guide for this exercise. Read it over a few times. Don't be in a hurry—feel free to focus on words or phrases through which you sense God speaking. Remind yourself that you don't have to be anywhere else or doing anything else.

Before you go any further, pray your own "search me" prayer. For example, *"Lord, help me right now to lower my defenses and trust your love. With the help of your Holy Spirit, what do I need to see? Search me . . . know me . . . point out any offenses . . ."*

In addition to just reading the psalm, consider actually speaking the words. Hear yourself saying out loud what is true from God's Word. Add your name in several places so it hits home that these words are meant for *you*—that God is personally speaking to you, about you.

The following questions are optional. Use them if they help focus your thoughts.

Search me . . .

1. According to verses 1–6 of Psalm 139, what specifically is God already fully aware of when it comes to your life?

Does knowing this evoke any emotions in you?

2. David was not afraid of God's scrutiny—he did not fear being judged, shamed, or rejected by God. Yet David certainly knew he was sinful. How is it possible for someone who has fallen short of God's standard not to fear God's close gaze? (See Ps. 32:1.)

Know my heart . . .

3. Jesus said our heart follows our treasure (Matt. 6:20−21, 24). What have you been treasuring these days?

4. According to Jesus, our words reveal our heart (Matt. 12:34)—more so than our intentions or sometimes even our actions. Think of the things you've said over the last week. What would an unbiased person conclude about your heart from these utterances?

Know my heart ...

5. What has your mind tended to drift toward in idle moments? Use the list below, or come up with your own word or phrase:

gratitude	jealousy	impatience	contentment
lust	envy	love	anger
joy	anxiety	greed	fear

See if there is any offensive way in me ...

6. The reading pointed out that sometimes we avoid praying the "search me" prayer because we *know* where the Holy Spirit's spotlight would go. Does that seem true for you? Are you currently aware of any offensive (hurtful) way in your life? How has that impacted your self-esteem, anxiety level, or spiritual progress? What would it take for you to make a fresh surrender—to let it go?

NOTE: If you've identified an issue, we strongly encourage you to share it with a trusted friend or Christian counselor. While that may feel frightening, significant change rarely happens in isolation. Transformation is fueled by openness and community.

7. What do you think it means to be led "in the way everlasting" in these areas?

"Stretch Me" Prayer

David was certainly no stranger to being stretched. As a king, he felt tremendous pressure from internal sources as well as matters of state. Yet he was willing to walk with God through it all, and willingly accepted challenges as an assignment from God—during which new opportunities to rely on God would present themselves.

Continuing in your meditation on Psalm 139, imagine ways in which the God who inspired these words might want to stretch you. What edges of your comfort zone may God want to gently but firmly push you past? What opportunities are present that God is calling you to enter into, and in which he could show his mighty power on your behalf?

You might pray, *"Lord I know you want the best for me. I want to become what you want me to become and to do whatever you ask. Here is how, by faith, I want you to stretch me ..."*

Again, the ideal would be for you to just meditate on the passage and on the "stretch me" prayer. But if you need direction, use some of the following optional questions.

1. Moses gives us a good example of someone struggling with being stretched. What stretching thing does God ask Moses to do in Exodus 3:9–10?

2. What is Moses' response? (Ex. 3:11; 4:10–13) What was he afraid of?

3. In what areas do you sense God may want to stretch you? This might involve something God is calling you to *do* (a new area of ministry, an adventure in evangelism, etc.) or this may involve who God is inviting you to *become* (see discussion of the fruit of the Spirit in Session 1). How do you find yourself responding to this?

4. As we've been saying, effort alone will probably not produce lasting changes in these areas. What training exercises or spiritual disciplines do you think could help bring a greater degree of growth in your life?

"Lead Me" Prayer

David required God's regular input. Important decisions affecting a whole nation could not be faced without the confidence that God would help. David turned to God again and again for leadership and direction.

David's God is saying to you, "Let me lead you." The One who knows when you sit and when you rise (Ps. 139:2), the One who has laid his hand upon you (v. 10), the One who delights to lead you in the way everlasting (v. 24) is ready to hear and answer your prayer for guidance.

You might want to pray, *"Lord, I have my hopes and dreams for my life, but ultimately only what you direct me to do will be best. I hold all these up to you now, and ask that you confirm or redirect. Specifically, I want you to lead me . . ."*

If you need help, use these optional questions.

1. What are some general principles of God's guidance taught in James 4:13–17?

2. Reflect on the past week. Did you take action on a small prompting from the Spirit? What was the result? Do you tend to second-guess these leadings?

3. Sometimes God's leading is clear, but it's difficult to follow. Can you think of a step God is asking you to take which is hard for you? What makes that difficult?

4. Proverbs 3:5–6 lays out some prior commitments to be made before God will lead us. What are those? Describe your own inclination recently regarding those commitments.

Review the Experience

Before you make the transition back into your daily activities, take a few minutes to reflect on what has just happened. What did you observe happening in yourself as you had this time of solitude? Did your mind wander? Did you talk to God about how hard it was to stay focused? Did it feel pleasant? What was the high point? When was it difficult? How would you summarize what happened if you had to tell someone about it right now?

TAKE-AWAY

My summary of the main point of this session, and how it impacts me personally:

NOTE: You will fill in this information after your group discussion. Leave it blank until the conclusion of your meeting.

SESSION
SIX

The Roundabout Way

Reading adapted from a message by John Ortberg

When you're going on a journey, if you have small children with you, there is one question you will inevitably face. The children will ask it. They will ask it soon. They will ask it often. They will ask it with a kind of whining, obstinate passion. They will ask it even though you warn them you never want to hear it again. It will be like nails on a blackboard.

"*Are we there yet?*"

Imagine going on a trip and saying, "We're not there yet. We won't get there today—or even tomorrow. In fact, our whole life is going to be a journey. We are headed for the one destination in the world worth traveling to, and we have wonderful assurances about our ultimate arrival—but we're not there yet."

> "*We're not there yet. We won't get there today—or even tomorrow. In fact, our whole life is going to be a journey.*"

The God of the Roundabout Way

The children of God were getting ready to go on a journey. They were going from slavery to freedom; from rags to riches; from Egypt to the Promised Land. It sounded like a very simple journey. They could not have expected it would take long. Once they left Egypt, all they had to do was to cross the Sinai Peninsula. It was less than two hundred miles. They could do it in a matter of weeks.

But God had an alternate route in mind. The text says that when Pharaoh let the people go, God did not lead them by way of the land of the Philistines, although that was nearer; for God thought, "If they face war, they might change their minds and return to Egypt" (Ex. 13:17). So God led the people by way of the wilderness.

This is the God who, precisely because he loves his children, refuses to take the shortcut they would have, no doubt, preferred. This is the roundabout way of God.

Imagine the whole nation of Israel setting out on their journey home. They are not worried about directions. They will be guided by God and his amazing pillar of fire. The pillar starts to move, the march begins. But then the people notice: It's going the wrong way! The Promised Land is northeast, and the pillar is headed south. The pillar is directionally challenged!

Will the people follow God even when they don't understand? Will they follow him when following doesn't seem to make any sense? Will they stay faithful on the roundabout way of God?

When God leads his people, he does not move hastily. He is never in a hurry.

When God leads his people, he does not move hastily. He is never in a hurry. It is one of his most irritating qualities. He is the God who takes his people to the Promised Land by way of the desert.

The Desert Experience

Israel would spend forty years on this roundabout way. Forty years in the desert. Forty is a significant number in Scripture. It is especially associated with the desert. When Moses killed an Egyptian and fled from Pharaoh, he lived in the desert forty years. When Elijah ran in fear from Jezebel, he was led into the wilderness for forty days and forty nights. And, of course, Jesus himself began his ministry with forty days of fasting and prayer in the desert.

Over and over it happens in the lives of those who seek God. Everybody is going to log some time in the desert. Life begins at forty.

Often, a journey to the desert is triggered by some event: a relationship shatters, a child rebels, you endure a financial disaster, a dream dies. But sometimes it comes for no discernible reason at all. The desert.

St. John of the Cross (a writer on spiritual life) wrote that a desert experience, or what he calls "the dark night of the soul," is often a part of a believer's experience not long after conversion. When you first become a Christian, God often gives a gift of pure spiritual desire. You have an appetite to know more about God. You long to pray. You arc hungry to read the Bible. Worship is alive. You don't want to sin.

It may be, if you're lucky, that you go on like this for fifty or sixty years and then die. It may be that your whole life will have been a straight line of spiritual growth. But for most of us, life does not work that way.

For most of us, somewhere along the line things change. What was once easy and enjoyable becomes more laborious. You pour your heart out to God, but there is no sense of response, no sense of nearness. The Bible feels dull. You are confused and you wonder why, but you receive no answer. Temptations you thought you had overcome begin to look good again. Faith itself is hard. Your spirit feels dry and barren. You are not just in the desert, the desert is *in you*. Have you ever felt this way? It *may* be the result of deliberate, ongoing sin. If so, you need to confess and repent. But often it seems to come out of the blue.

The desert is where you face the question of perseverance.

The Desert as the Place of Endurance

It would be nice if the desert were a one-time-only experience, like getting vaccinated or having your wisdom teeth pulled. But the desert is a place we return to again and again.

The desert is where you face the question of perseverance. It is easy to trust in the land of milk and honey when everything's working out right. When prayers get answered and problems go away and the kids' teeth are straight, faith is not hard. But the desert has a way of building strength.

In the desert, only the patient can go on. Will you follow the pillar again today? Will you continue to follow when all positive feelings are gone? The desert is the place where you learn to obey when obeying is no longer easy. When you grow to give thanks even in the desert, you are growing strong. When you are on the roundabout way but say, "I won't go back to Egypt; I will be faithful; I will endure," *then* you are growing mighty in your soul.

The Desert Is the Place of God's Love

As odd as it sounds, the desert can offer a unique opportunity to experience the depth of God's love. In the desert, the work of God's love can speak to a deeper place in your heart. You come to God and you haven't prayed well—or maybe at all; you have been battered by temptation, rocked by doubt. You feel you may be more hindrance than help to whatever work God may be doing in the world. Yet even so, you hear the words: "I still love you. I could not love you more than I do now. I still want you for my child. Haven't you learned? You are the object of my undying affection. You are the beloved."

To be loved when we are feeling unlovely, unlovable—that's life to someone who's dying. That's grace.

To be loved when we are feeling lovable—that's good. To be loved when we are feeling unlovely, unlovable—that's life to someone who's dying. That's grace.

The desert really was intended to be a place where God could be present with his people, so they could come to know and trust him. In the desert there were no great cities to build, no great battles to win—just God and his people. He would feed them every morning when they ate, guide them every day when they walked, and protect them every night when they slept. The desert was intended by God to be life beyond achievement. It was to be a life of love.

On the roundabout way, there may be questions that don't get answered and confusion that does not lift. Still, one must choose. Is there hope on this roundabout way? Can even a barren place lead to life? Is it a cul-de-sac or does it finally lead, after all the twists and turns, to home?

Are you in the desert now? If not, you may be soon. Remember, God has not forgotten you. You have not been abandoned. It may not be the quickest way or the easiest way. But God is at work in the roundabout way of the desert. Ultimately, he is not nearly as concerned with *where* his people are going as *who they will be* when they get there.

Are we there yet?

Not yet. One day, but not yet. In the meantime, be patient and let God work in his roundabout way.

This week there are two options. If you are walking through a desert right now, use the first exercise. If not, skip to the second exercise on the next page.

A Desert Prayer

One of the most significant things we can do when we're in the wilderness is summed up in a single word: *wait*. Isaiah wrote: "Those who wait for the LORD shall renew their strength" (Isa. 40:31 NRSV). Sometimes *waiting* is all you can do—and the best thing to do. Consider this:

> *I would like to offer one more counsel to those who find themselves devoid of the presence of God. It is this: wait on God. Wait, silent and still. Wait, attentive and responsive. Learn that trust precedes faith. Faith is a little like putting your car into gear, and right now you cannot exercise faith, you cannot move forward. Do not berate yourself for this. But when you are unable to put your spiritual life into drive, do not put it into reverse; put it into neutral. Trust is how you put your spiritual life in neutral. Trust is confidence in the character of God. Firmly and deliberately you say, "I do not understand what God is doing or even where God is, but I know that he is out to do me good." This is trust. This is how to wait.*
>
> —Richard Foster, *Prayer: Finding the Heart's True Home*

This week, try taking this simple prayer with you through your wilderness: *Lord, I will wait on you.*

Also consider these steps:

- Share your dryness or confusion with another person.
- Ask a few trusted friends for sustained prayer.
- Don't try to force feelings of spiritual vitality. (But don't go "back to Egypt" and its destructive patterns either!)
- Allow for some change. Modify your pace, your daily routines, even your usual spiritual disciplines to allow for some freshness.

- Consider getting more rest and recreation. Deliberately seek out some "green pastures" and "still waters" (Ps. 23:2).
- Find things—even small things—to give thanks for. Notice tokens of God's grace to you even though you're not out of the hard place yet.
- Finally, don't panic. Even if you don't feel him, God is still with you and working for your good.

If You're Not in the Desert Right Now . . .

One of the reasons that times in the wilderness seem so foreign and difficult is that few of us today have much capacity for deprivation or trials. In our culture, we are accustomed to direct routes. We like efficiency. We value ease. We prize convenience. This is what we consider *normal*. Anything else feels *abnormal*. It's no wonder that God's roundabout ways seem so uncomfortable and that the desert becomes something to *flee* from instead of to *learn* from.

But there is a way to train for times in the desert. Small trials can be used to prepare us. Consider using the following day-to-day hassles to train yourself in qualities like patience, endurance, trust, and waiting.

- Experiencing interruptions
- Encountering annoying people
- Not getting your desires met
- Being unfairly criticized or misunderstood
- Needing to set aside your preferences for someone else
- Experiencing frustrating delays
- Feeling unappreciated

How did the Spirit speak to you through these experiences? What did your responses tell you about what was in your heart—just below the surface—as the experiences occurred? What practices and attitudes made these experiences more tolerable, or even positive? Of what training benefit were they?

1. According to John 10:10, what is Jesus' intent for every believer?

   How do you understand this promise given the reality of desert times?

2. Considering your own desert experiences, is there any way that something dry, barren, and painful can lead to something abundant or full of life?

3. Though we may intellectually know that God is at work through the desert times of our lives, why is it still so difficult to go through them?

What are the core issues and emotions that make those times so hard for you?

4. What negative attitudes or behaviors are you most susceptible to when you go through desert-wandering periods in your life?

5. Consider these words of Richard Foster as he speaks of a time in the wilderness he endured:

For me the greatest value in my lack of control was the intimate and ultimate awareness that I could not manage God. God refused to jump when I said, "Jump!" Neither by theological acumen nor by religious technique could I conquer God. God was, in fact, to conquer me.

—*Prayer: Finding the Heart's True Home*

How have your own desert times confronted you with your desire to control your life? Control others? Control God?

What was the outcome of those attempts?

Do you sense any way in which God is lovingly conquering you (and your controlling tendencies) through these difficult times?

6. What is your understanding of what James meant by *perseverance (or endurance)* in James 1:2–4?

What areas of life are especially helped when people have developed this character strength?

7. Paul paints a pretty grim picture of his life in 2 Corinthians 4:7–12. Yet even though he describes dark scenes, there is a hopeful thread throughout. Put in your own words the essence of that positive aspect of Paul's experiences.

To what extent is a similar hope present in you?

What do you think you need in order for your life story to be written with that same positive emphasis?

8. Hebrews 12:1–2 speaks of running the race with perseverance. What are we to lay aside in order to do so?

What might that be for you personally?

What do you think it means to fix your eyes on Jesus?

9. What additional light do these passages from the book of Hebrews shed on why we can take comfort from fixing our eyes on Jesus during desert times?

2:17–18

4:15–16

5:8–9

10. Close this study by reading God's reassuring words to his people in Isaiah 40:28–31. Rewrite those words as if he is speaking directly to you.

Take some time to prayerfully apply these promises in light of your current situation.

TAKE-AWAY

My summary of the main point of this session, and how it impacts me personally:

NOTE: You will fill in this information after your group discussion. Leave it blank until the conclusion of your meeting.

SESSION SEVEN

And the Greatest of These Is Love

Reading adapted from a message by John Ortberg

B ob is a leader in the Christian community. Everyone admires his impressive command of Scripture. He views himself as a "defender of truth" and regularly opposes others who disagree with his doctrinal positions. In truth, he doesn't just oppose them; he *delights* in opposing them. He attacks them. He ridicules their positions and maligns their motives. When he listens to sermons, it is not to encounter God or be broken but to point out flaws. *He is regarded as a spiritual giant. But he does not know love.*

He is regarded as a spiritual giant. But he does not know love.

Helen is a veteran Christian, a founding member of her church—and one of the most feared persons in it. People tiptoe around her, skillfully avoiding her critical words. These days, she is especially critical of the changes that are opening her church to new people. She has little tolerance for those outside the church—people who don't look, think, act, dress, or vote like she does. *She is seen as a mature believer. But she does not know love.*

It takes a daily planner the size of Montana to organize all of Jerry's church meetings and activities. People marvel at his commitment and amazing capacity to manage so many ministry involvements. In the church he is known by everyone—but no one *really* knows him. For years, his marriage has been dry and devoid of intimacy. His children cannot speak freely with him and feel little affection from him. His closest friends feel they barely know the man behind all the ministry. *He is a faithful churchman. But he does not know love.*

What's troubling is not that such people exist. God knows I have weaknesses as great as these. What's troubling is not that such people exist in the church. The church is a place for people with weaknesses. What's most troubling is that in church after church, they are looked up to as examples of what it means to be spiritually mature.

The Centrality of Love

Spirituality—spiritual growth—wrongly understood is death. It produces people that are prideful, judgmental, exclusive, unable to love—people with cold hearts, plastic masks, inauthentic lives, and shriveled souls.

Spiritual growth rightly understood is a life of wonder, joy, worship, gratitude, servanthood, humility, courage, truth. But always there is one central characteristic. Love.

Spiritual growth rightly understood? It is many things. It is a life of wonder, joy, worship, gratitude, servanthood, humility, courage, truth. But always there is one central characteristic: *love.*

> *Love the Lord your God with all your heart and with all your soul and with all your mind and with all your strength. . . . Love your neighbor as yourself.*
>
> —Mark 12:30–31

> *If I have the gift of prophecy and can fathom all mysteries and all knowledge, and if I have a faith that can move mountains, but have not love, I am nothing.*
>
> —1 Corinthians 13:2

> *Whoever does not love does not know God, because God is love.*
>
> —1 John 4:8

Love is God's signature. Is it ours?

Love and Grace

In a world of fallen people, love cannot exist for long without grace. Grace is the Bible's word for the strength that allows God to continue loving in the face of rejection, unworthiness, unloveliness. Grace is what allows love to be hurt, but keep forgiving; to be rejected, but keep hoping; to see potential goodness that lies buried beneath a crusty surface. Grace is the oxygen that love needs to breathe, the beating heart that keeps love alive.

Writers like Philip Yancy and Gordon MacDonald have pondered the question: "What is the one thing the church has to offer that the world cannot get anywhere else?" You don't have to be a Christian to build homes for the homeless or feed the poor. You don't have to be a Christian to try to effect political change or pass social legislation. There are other religions whose teachers offer wise moral instruction. What's the one thing that the church has to offer that the world cannot get anywhere else? *Grace.*

Living in grace, remembering grace, keeps love alive. Losing touch with grace, forgetting that I am loved only because God is a gracious God—that is a love-killer. And the world is tired of Christians who proclaim the right beliefs and are committed to the right values but in whom there is no love, in whom there is no grace.

What's the one thing that the church has to offer that the world cannot get anywhere else? Grace.

The Way It's Supposed to Be

Victor Hugo's *Les Miserables* is the story of the triumph of grace. The paroled convict Jean Valjean, imprisoned for twenty years because he stole a loaf of bread, is shown hospitality in the home of a bishop. But temptation is too much. He takes the bishop's silver and steals away into the night. Stopped by a constable, he tries to lie his way out of trouble: "The silver was a gift," he says. The constable takes him back to the bishop and Jean Valjean waits to hear the words that will return him to prison until he dies. Nothing in his life prepared him for what he is about to hear.

"You are mistaken," the bishop says to Valjean. "Of course this silver is my gift. But only part. You forgot to take the candlesticks."

Jean Valjean waits for the condemnation he knows he deserves. Instead he is blindsided by grace. One moment he faces poverty and prison; the next, freedom and abundance.

But the bishop tells him one more thing before he leaves: "You must never forget this moment. Your soul, your life, have been bought back. You are not your own. From now on, you belong to God." And because of grace, Jean Valjean's life becomes an act of love. Honoring the promise given to a dying prostitute, he devotes himself to raising her child, Cosette. Later he jeopardizes his own life and freedom to save the man who loves Cosette.

Opposed to Valjean is a man committed to the law—to spirituality wrongly understood. The constable Jauvert is convinced of his own righteousness. An eye for an eye, a tooth for a tooth, he is a champion of morality and justice. He spends his life seeking to re-imprison Valjean.

Let us give Jauvert his day in court. He believes in many good things. He is committed to truth. He wants wrongdoing stamped out. He desires a society without thievery, deceit, or corruption. He makes personal sacrifices to pursue such a society. He sincerely believes he is an agent of good.

"Your soul, your life, have been bought back. You are not your own. From now on, you belong to God."

But in his world there is no room for grace. And because he is blind to his own need for grace, his capacity to love withers and dies. He cannot offer mercy. The crisis of his existence occurs when Jean Valjean risks his own life to save the life of Jauvert, his relentless pursuer. But Jauvert cannot bring himself to receive that grace. He kills himself rather than to admit the truth—that his own sin has been as great as that of the man he devoted his life to punishing.

In the end it is Valjean, the convict, who is able to love. He comes to see what is expressed so beautifully in the musical—to love another person is to see the face of God.

This is the church the way it's supposed to be. This is spiritual growth the way it's supposed to be. People caught holding the silver. People blindsided by grace. People who still hear the words, "Your soul, your life, have been bought back. You are not your own. From now on, you belong to God." People whose lives, because of grace, become an act of love.

" . . . and the greatest of these is love."

God's Signature Is Love

As you go through your week, make a point of noticing the concrete ways God's "signature" is evidenced in your life—acts of grace, kindness, daily provision, protection, refreshment, etc. Discipline yourself to *notice*. Try to have eyes to see what you might ordinarily take for granted. Consider keeping a running list.

Is Your Signature Love?

Take the phrase "the greatest of these is love" with you throughout the week. Let it be your companion. As you study 1 Corinthians 13 in the Bible study, let the words wash you, guide you. Let them shape each encounter that you have—with family, friends, in the church, in the marketplace, in the grocery store, at the gas station—the significant ones and the seemingly insignificant ones.

As you leave a particular encounter, pause to ask yourself, "Did that person in any way feel God's signature of love through me?"

When you fail, acknowledge that, receive God's forgiving grace, and realize that another opportunity will come along.

Keep a record of how this experience goes for you. What difference did it make in the way you went about your day? When did it come easily? When was it most difficult? When was it complex or confusing?

1. What are the behaviors or achievements Paul notes in 1 Corinthians 13:1–3 that, when done without love, amount to nothing?

   Is Paul overstating his case? Explain.

2. Imagine for a moment that Paul is writing to *you*. Rewrite verses 1–3 with what you are occasionally (or even frequently) tempted to elevate over love?

3. *"Everything,* if there is no love, is *nothing."* Do you agree with that statement? Why do you think we sometimes give in to spirituality wrongly understood—and fruitlessly pursue activities or accomplishments that are not born from love and do not result in love?

4. In 1 Corinthians 13:4–7, Paul uses fifteen words to characterize love. Read this passage in at least two different translations, and then, in your own words, summarize the qualities of love.

5. First Corinthians 13:4–7 was absolutely true of Jesus. In fact, you can replace the word "love" with "Jesus" and make perfect sense of this passage. Describe below some of the ways Jesus has manifested these different aspects of love to you personally.

6. Now replace the word "love" in each of the statements (vv. 4–7) with your own name. Actually write those verses down here:

Note in what ways, in the last few weeks, you've seen yourself manifesting these aspects of love.

7. In the above instances, what enabled you to respond in loving ways? (Examples: I was slowed down enough to see the need and step in; I was rested, so I had energy to help; a Scripture passage that I had been "living with" prompted my actions.)

8. Which, if any, of the above statements with your name attached cause you to wince?

Describe specifically how you may have failed to show love. What contributed to your inability to be loving in those instances?

9. In the reading, Valjean represented a man overwhelmed by grace, and Jauvert was concerned with law. Who are you most like these days? What is causing that emphasis?

10. Reflect on what you have been studying and experiencing throughout this entire study on spiritual growth. What connection are you seeing between *training* (engaging in practices that keep you connected to Christ) and being a more loving person?

11. When all is said and done, according to John 15:1–10, what one thing is ultimately required of you if you are serious about pursuing a life of growth and a life of love?

TAKE-AWAY

My summary of the main point of this session, and how it impacts me personally:

NOTE: You will fill in this information after your group discussion. Leave it blank until the conclusion of your meeting.

Leader's Guide

How to Use This Discussion Guide

Doers of the Word

One of the reasons small groups are so effective is because when people are face-to-face, they can discuss and process information instead of merely listening passively. *God's truths are transforming only to the extent they are received and absorbed.* Just as uneaten food cannot nourish, truth "out there" — either in a book or spoken by a teacher — cannot make a difference if it is undigested. Even if it is bitten off and chewed, it must be swallowed and made part of each cell to truly give life.

The spiritual transformation at the heart of this Bible study series can occur only if people get truth and make that truth part of their lives. Reading about sit-ups leaves you flabby; doing sit-ups gives you strong abdominals. That's why in every session, we present group members with exercises to do during the week. They also study Scripture on their own in (hopefully) unhurried settings where they can meditate on and ponder the truths that are encountered. Group discussion is the other way we've designed for them to grab hold of these important lessons.

This study is not a correspondence course. It's a personal and group experience designed to help believers find a biblical approach to their spiritual lives that really works. We recognize that people have a variety of learning styles, so we've tried to incorporate a variety of ways to learn. One of the most important ways they will learn is when they meet together to process the information verbally in a group.

Not Question-by-Question

One approach to learning used by some small groups encourages members to systematically discuss *everything* they learn on their own during the group time. Such material is designed so group members do a study and then report what their answers were for each question. While this approach is thorough, it can become boring. The method we've adopted includes individual study, but we do not suggest discussing *everything* in the session when you meet. Instead, questions are given to leaders (hence, this Leader's Guide) to get at the heart of the material without being rote recitations of the answers the members came up with on their own. This may be a bit confusing at first, because some people fill in the blanks, expecting each answer to be discussed, and discussed in the order they wrote them down. Instead, you, as a leader, will be asking questions *based* on their study, but not necessarily numerically corresponding to their study. We think this technique of handling the sessions has the best of both approaches: individual learning is reinforced in the group setting without becoming wearisome.

It is also important that you understand you will not be able to cover all the material provided each week. We give you more than you can use in every session—not to frustrate you, but to give you enough so you can pick and choose. *Base your session plan on the needs of individual members of your group.*

There may be a few times when the material is so relevant to your group members that every question seems to fit. Don't feel bad about taking two weeks on a session. The purpose of this series is transformational life-change, not timely book completion!

Getting Ready for *Your* Group

We suggest that to prepare for a meeting, you first do the study yourself and spend some time doing the spiritual exercise. Then look over the questions we've given you in the Leader's Guide. As you consider your group members and the amount of discussion time you have, ask yourself if the questions listed for that session relate to your group's needs. Would some other questions fit better? We've tried to highlight the main points of each session, but you may feel you need to hit some aspect harder than we did, or not spend as much time on a point. As long as your preparation is based on knowledge of your group, customize the session however you see fit.

As we pointed out, you may have to adapt the material because of time considerations. It is very hard to discuss every topic in a given session in detail—we certainly don't recommend it. You may also only have a limited time because of the nature of your group. Again, the purpose isn't to cover every question exhaustively, but to get the main point across in each session (whatever incidental discussion may otherwise occur). As a guide to your preparation, review the *Primary Focus* statement at the beginning and the *Session Highlights* paragraph at the end of each session's Leader's Guide. They represent our attempt to summarize what we were trying to get across in writing the sessions. If your questions get at those points, you're on the right track.

A Guide, Not a Guru

Now a word about your role as leader. We believe all small groups need a leader. While it is easy to see that a group discussion would get off track without a facilitator, we would like you to ponder another very important reason you hold the position you do.

This Bible study series is about spiritual growth—about Christ being formed in each of us. One of the greatest gifts you can give another person is to pay attention to his or her spiritual life. As a leader, you will serve your group members by observing their lives and trying to hear, in the questions they ask and the answers they give, where they are in their spiritual development. Your discerning observations are an invaluable contribution to their spiritual progress. That attention, prayer, and insight is an extremely rare gift—but it is revolutionary for those blessed enough to have such a person in their lives. You are that person. You give that gift. You can bring that blessing.

People desperately need clarity about spirituality. Someone needs to blow away the fog that surrounds the concept of what it means to live a spiritual life and give believers concrete ideas how to pursue it. Spiritual life is just *life*. It's that simple. Christ-followers must invite God into all aspects of life, even the everyday routines. That is where we spend most of our time anyway, so that is where we must be with God. If not, the Christian life will become pretense, or hypocrisy. We must decompartmentalize life so that we share it all with God in a barrier-free union with him.

We say all this so that you, the leader, can be encouraged in and focused on your role. You are the person observing how people are doing. You are the one who detects the doors people will not let God through, the one who sees the blind spots they don't, the one who gently points out the unending patience of God who will not stop working in us until "his work is completed" (Phil. 1:6). You will hold many secret conversations with God about the people in your group—while you meet, during a phone call, sitting across the table at lunch, when you're alone. In addition to making the meeting happen, this is one of the most important things you can do to be a catalyst for life-change. That is why you're meeting together anyway—to see people become more like Christ. If you lead as a *facilitator* of discussion, not a teacher, and a *listener* rather than the one who should be listened to, you will see great changes in the members of your group.

Training to Live Like Jesus

Primary Focus: To understand that pursuing spiritual transformation involves training, not just trying.

Remember that these questions do not correspond numerically with the questions in the assignment. We do not recommend simply going over what your group members put for their answers—that will probably result in a tedious discussion at best. Rather, use these questions (and perhaps some of your own) to stimulate discussion; that way, you'll be processing the content of the lesson from a fresh perspective each meeting.

1. Based on the exercise, what experience this week helped you train to be more like Jesus? How did this experience help you?

2. What did you think of the parallels between sailing and living the Christian life as described in the reading? Describe an area in your life you are trying to handle through willpower alone, where you can make an application of this principle.

3. *(Regarding question 3 in the Bible study)* What is your understanding of what it means to *abide* (or *remain*) in Jesus? What questions do you have about how to do this practically?

4. *(Regarding question 5 in the Bible study)* What do you see as the connection between training and abiding? What insight did 1 Corinthians 9:24–27 give you regarding why learning to abide is not a passive activity?

5. What spiritual practices are a regular part of your life? How are these working for you?

6. What activities are you tempted to view as "fruitful Christian living" but are not really leading to you being more Christlike? What does this tell you about your deeper assumptions and attitudes about spirituality?

7. Talk about two or three aspects of the fruit of the Spirit exercise and where you placed your current expression of that fruit.

How did you feel as you rated yourself? What new resolve (or discouragement) are you walking around with these days?

8. *(Regarding question 8 in the Bible study)* In what areas were you affirmed about what God is doing in you? In what areas are you looking for greater transformation?

Take-Away: At the conclusion of your discussion each week, take a few minutes to have group members sum up the session and its impact on them by filling in the Take-Away section at the end of each session. Don't tell them what they are supposed to write— let them be true to their own experiences. When they have written their summaries, have everyone share with the others what they wrote. Statements should be similar to the statements in Session Highlights. If you feel the whole group may have missed an important aspect of the session, be sure to bring that up in the closing discussion.

Session Highlights: Willpower alone won't change me; I must enter into a life of training. Certain practices are foundational to spiritual life (prayer, Bible study, and solitude); ordinary moments are also the laboratory for life-change.

NOTE: In Session 2, the spiritual exercise follows the Bible study. Alert your group members to this so that they allow enough time to complete the Bible study and engage in the exercise before your next meeting.

SESSION TWO

The Practice of Scripture Meditation

Primary Focus: To allow the Bible to wash through us as a means of transformation.

1. What was the phrase you wrote down to take with you throughout the week for your spiritual exercise? How did that influence your week?

2. As you meditated on and prayed through the Lord's Prayer, what was the most meaningful part?

3. What tends to keep you from using Scripture to be spiritually transformed?

> NOTE: Some possible answers . . .
>
> • Don't read it at all (or rarely)
> • Read it for theological "ammo"
> • Read it mechanically as an assignment to complete

4. What do you think of when you hear the phrase "meditating on the Scriptures"? Are you uncomfortable with any aspect of this? Explain.

> NOTE: Meditation does not have to be spooky. It is simply the practice of "sustained attention." We all do this kind of thinking almost every day, but we tend to be careless and don't have a worthy focus. The purpose of biblical meditation is to choose God and his truth as the subject of our attention. The Scriptures command us to do this, so we need to make this practice a priority.

5. *(Regarding question 1 in the Bible study)* What were the praying errors Jesus mentioned in Matthew 6? What pulls you (or others you know) toward those errors?

6. *(Regarding question 6 in the Bible study)* What spiritual parallels exist between the children of Israel gathering manna and our praying for daily bread?

7. *(Regarding question 7 in the Bible study)* What did you think of the two statements? Is there a person in your life right now who you're having trouble forgiving? Explain.

8. How would you like to apply this practice of slowly going through the Scriptures in the coming weeks? What problems do you anticipate in doing this?

Session Highlights: The goal of Bible reading, studying, and meditation is not to get through the Word but to let the Word get through me; the Word must wash me, and it can't be done quickly; a growing knowledge of the Bible is important, but it's better to have a small understanding with obedience than lots of knowledge without transformation.

SESSION THREE

The Practice of Solitude

Primary Focus: To learn to value and engage in solitude.

1. How susceptible are you to "hurry sickness"? What did you observe during the week as you deliberately sought to "ruthlessly eliminate hurry from your life"?

2. What has been your experience with solitude in the past? What do you like about it? Dislike? Why is solitude with lots of input from books, tapes, and music missing the point?

3. What is your understanding of the difference between being busy and being hurried? What drives you personally toward hurry?

4. What is your opinion of this statement: "Hurry is evidence of a disordered heart, not a disordered schedule." How have you seen hurry affect your spiritual life adversely (such as your ability to love, to listen to God, to feel love, to be fully present with people, etc.)?

5. *(Regarding question 6 in the Bible study)* Why was Mary commended? What was Martha missing?

6. *(Regarding question 7 in the Bible study)* What needs did solitude meet for Jesus?

7. What changes would happen for you if you got more intentional about solitude? What stands in the way of you practicing solitude more frequently?

Session Highlights: I must ruthlessly eliminate hurry from my life. I can be busy, but hurry is a disease of my heart. Solitude is important not only to eliminate hurriedness, but also to be in a place to hear God and allow him to form me spiritually.

SESSION FOUR

Simple Prayer

Primary Focus: To accept the imperfections of our prayers, but to pray anyway.

> NOTE: It may be good for the group to spend some time together in simple prayer. Be sure to allow enough time for this.

1. What did you observe as you tried keeping a running conversation with God this week? Did you sense any breakthroughs?

2. Describe the general condition of your prayer life. Historically for you, what has been the hardest part about prayer (such as boredom, mind-wandering, fatigue, distorted view of God, guilt about prayerlessness)?

3. *(Regarding questions 5 and 6 in the Bible study)* How does the "negotiating" by Moses and Abraham with God compare with your own prayer experiences? What causes you to shrink back from such bold praying?

4. *(Regarding question 7 in the Bible study)* Do you have a hard time bringing your complaints to God? What kept David from becoming stuck in bitterness? What helps you during these types of seasons?

5. *(Regarding question 8 in the Bible study)* What observations can you make about Jesus' prayer life toward the end of his life? Do any of these statements surprise or trouble you? What application can you make to your own prayer life from his example?

6. What is the difference between boldness in prayer and arrogance? What is the difference between respect toward God and cowering?

Session Highlights: I must come to God just as I am in prayer; it's okay to stumble around, to pray "poorly," to be confused, as long as we press on and pray; even our prayerlessness and struggles can be subjects of prayer.

> NOTE: In next week's session, the Bible study and exercise are combined into a single solitude experience. This will optimally require setting aside a block of several hours. Alert your group of this in advance. If it is not possible for someone to set aside that amount of time, the "Three Prayers" exercise can be done in three separate sittings.

A Word about Leadership: Remember the comments at the beginning of this discussion guide about your role as a leader? About now, it's probably a good idea to remind yourself that one of your key functions is to be a cheerleader—someone who seeks out signs of spiritual progress in others and makes some noise about it.

What have you seen God doing in your group members' lives as a result of this study? Don't assume that they've seen that progress—and definitely don't assume they are beyond needing simple words of encouragement. Find ways to point out to people the growth you've seen. Let them know it's happening, and that it's noticeable to you and others.

There aren't a whole lot of places in this world where people's spiritual progress is going to be recognized and celebrated. After all, wouldn't you like to hear someone cheer *you* on? So would your group members. You have the power to make a profound impact through a sincere, insightful remark.

Be aware, also, that some groups get sidetracked by a difficult member or situation that hasn't been confronted. And some individuals *could* be making significant progress—they just need a nudge. Encouragement is not about just saying nice things; it's about offering *words that urge*. It's about giving courage (en-*courage*-ment) to those who lack it.

So, take a risk. Say what needs to be said to encourage your members toward their goal of becoming fully devoted followers.

Three Transforming Prayers

Primary Focus: To experience the transformation that comes from the "search me," "stretch me," and "lead me" prayers.

1. Which of these three prayers seems the most important for you these days? Why?

2. Regarding the "search me" prayer: How does the thought of God searching you affect you?

3. What do your expenditures, your words, and your thoughts tell you about the condition of your heart lately? Did the Holy Spirit shine his light on an area of your life that clearly needs attention? If you feel it's appropriate, share that with the group.

4. Regarding the "stretch me" prayer: What is the comfort zone you most fear having to leave? In what area do you dread allowing God's presence?

5. Which training exercises or disciplines can help you cultivate progress in the fruit of the Spirit with which you need the most help?

6. Regarding the "lead me" prayer: What is an area of your life in which you are seeking God's guidance?

7. How easy is it for you to hear and respond to God's small promptings?

8. What is your overall trust level toward God these days? Where would you like to be able to trust him more?

Session Highlights: When the Holy Spirit searches, stretches, and leads you, it may be painful, but it is worth it. We must be willing to take a risk in prayer before we see results. Risky prayers reveal the extent of our trust in God.

SESSION SIX

The Roundabout Way

Primary Focus: To understand that the desert is a normal part of the spiritual experience and learn how to grow from it.

1. These days, are you more on the outside looking in at the desert or in the middle of the desert looking out? Explain.

2. Sometimes it can be helpful to know the cause of a desert experience. Are you able to discern the cause of your desert? What is it?

NOTE: When folks are in the desert, it can be helpful to ask some diagnostic questions. Dryness might be caused by something that's preventable or at least changeable; of course, it may not, and people do not need to feel guilty if they have trouble identifying a specific source. Consider these questions:

- Is there pain in my life that I need to feel and allow God to comfort me?
- Am I getting adequate rest?
- Is there unaddressed sin going on in my life?
- Am I in the midst of depression?
- Am I isolating myself from others? (Could God be calling me to more community in this desert?)
- Have I recently experienced a loss (relational, health, vocational, dream, etc.) I need to grieve?
- Is this simply a time for hanging on to God, to grow deeper, and not have any answers for now?

---

3. What is difficult for you to accept about the idea that desert experiences are a normal part of spiritual life?

4. If you had been one of the people of Israel wandering in the desert, what would you have thought or said as you saw the pillar of fire leading in such baffling directions? Share a time when your life was similarly confusing for a while.

5. For those in the desert: What does waiting on the Lord mean for you these days? What support can people offer that is helpful for you?

For those not in the desert: What small trials did you experience and learn from this week? What are the most helpful ways you can reach out to someone you know who is in a dry place?

6. *(Regarding question 7 in the Bible study)* Why do you think Paul was able to be positive even in the midst of his pain?

7. *(Regarding question 9 in the Bible study)* What is one thing from any of these passages that was helpful for you personally?

8. What new appreciation for the value of desert experiences are you taking away from the reading, study, or discussion?

Session Highlights: Desert times happen and can be learning experiences. We are accustomed to direct routes (efficiency), but God works in his own time through his own means. We can train for desert experiences even if we're not in them.

NOTE: When your group meeting ends, it may be meaningful for group members to gather around and offer prayer and encouragement to those currently experiencing the desert. Consider other ways to offer support through the week (notes, phone calls, etc.).

And the Greatest of These Is Love

Primary Focus: To recognize and commit to the centrality of love.

1. Did you notice God's signature of love throughout the week? Tell the group about a time you saw it.

2. Did you see love as your own signature throughout the week? Tell the group about a success story of your own.

3. *(Regarding question 2 in the Bible study)* What aspects of outward spiritual maturity are you prone to elevate above love? Have you known or admired (or feared) someone with such qualities? Why do you think you sometimes emphasize those secondary features above love?

4. *(Regarding question 3 in the Bible study)* What was your reaction to the statement, *"Everything*, if there is no love, is *nothing"*?

5. *(Regarding question 7 in the Bible study)* What barriers (such as fear, fatigue, hurry, anger, self-centeredness) keep you from responding in loving ways? What practices help you overcome those blocks?

6. *(Regarding question 9 in the Bible study)* These days are you more like Valjean (overwhelmed by grace) or Jauvert (concerned with law)? Why?

7. What do you believe is the key, for you personally, to becoming a person of deep love at every level—like Jesus? How can the group members help you on your journey?

Session Highlights: Everything, without love, is nothing; I must guard against any other superficial measure of spiritual maturity; when I see the extent of God's grace to me, it will help me be more loving; there are practices and experiences I can engage in to train me to be more loving over time.

John C. Ortberg Jr. is teaching pastor at Willow Creek Community Church in South Barrington, Illinois. He is the author of *The Life You've Always Wanted* and *Love Beyond Reason*. John and his wife, Nancy, live in the Chicago area with their three children, Laura, Mallory, and Johnny.

Laurie Pederson, a real estate investment manager, is a founding member of Willow Creek Community Church. As an elder since 1978, she has helped shape many of the foundational values and guiding principles of the church. She is cocreator of Willow Creek's discipleship-based church membership process. Laurie lives outside of Chicago with her husband, Scott.

Judson Poling, a staff member at Willow Creek Community Church since 1980, writes small group training materials and many of the dramas performed in Willow Creek's outreach services. He is coauthor of the *Walking with God* and *Tough Questions* Bible study series and general editor of *The Journey: A Study Bible for Spiritual Seekers*. He lives in Algonquin, Illinois, with his wife, Deb, and their two children, Anna and Ryan.

Willow Creek Association

Vision, Training, Resources for Prevailing Churches

This resource was created to serve you and to help you build a local church that prevails. It is just one of many ministry tools that are part of the Willow Creek Resources® line, published by the Willow Creek Association together with Zondervan.

The Willow Creek Association (WCA) was created in 1992 to serve a rapidly growing number of churches from across the denominational spectrum that are committed to helping unchurched people become fully devoted followers of Christ. Membership in the WCA now numbers over 10,500 Member Churches worldwide from more than ninety denominations.

The Willow Creek Association links like-minded Christian leaders with each other and with strategic vision, training, and resources in order to help them build prevailing churches designed to reach their redemptive potential. Here are some of the ways the WCA does that.

- **A2: Building Prevailing Acts 2 Churches—Today**—an annual two-and-a-half day event, held at Willow Creek Community Church in South Barrington, Illinois, to explore strategies for building churches that reach out to seekers and build believers, and to discover new innovations and breakthroughs from Acts 2 churches around the country.

- **The Leadership Summit**—a once a year, two-and-a-half-day conference to envision and equip Christians with leadership gifts and responsibilities. Presented live at Willow Creek as well as via satellite broadcast to over one hundred locations across North America, this event is designed to increase the leadership effectiveness of pastors, ministry staff, volunteer church leaders, and Christians in the marketplace.

- **Ministry-Specific Conferences**—throughout each year the WCA hosts a variety of conferences and training events—both at Willow Creek's main campus and offsite, across the U.S., and around the world—targeting church leaders and volunteers in ministry-specific areas such as: evangelism, small groups, preaching and teaching, the arts, children, students, women, volunteers, stewardship, raising up resources, etc.

- **Willow Creek Resources®**—provides churches with trusted and field-tested ministry resources in such areas as leadership, evangelism, spiritual formation, spiritual gifts, small groups, stewardship, student ministry, children's ministry, the use of the arts-drama, media, contemporary music —and more.

- **WCA Member Benefits**—includes substantial discounts to WCA training events, a 20 percent discount on all Willow Creek Resources®, *Defining Moments* monthly audio journal for leaders, quarterly *Willow* magazine, access to a Members-Only section on WillowNet, monthly communications, and more. Member Churches also receive special discounts and premier services through WCA's growing number of ministry partners—Select Service Providers—and save an average of $500 annually depending on the level of engagement.

For specific information about WCA conferences, resources, membership, and other ministry services contact:

Willow Creek Association
P.O. Box 3188
Barrington, IL 60011-3188
Phone: 847-570-9812
Fax: 847-765-5046
www.willowcreek.com

a place where ...

nobody stands alone!

Small groups, when they're working right, provide a place where you can experience continuous growth and community—the deepest level of community, modeled after the church in Acts 2, where believers are devoted to Christ's teachings and to fellowship with each other.

If you'd like to take the next step in building that kind of small group environment for yourself or for your church, we'd like to help.

The Willow Creek Association in South Barrington, Illinois, hosts an annual Small Groups Conference attended by thousands of church and small group leaders from around the world. Each year we also lead small group training events and workshops in seven additional cities across the country. We offer a number of small group resources for both small groups and small group leaders available to you through your local bookstore and Willow Creek Resources.

If you'd like to learn more, contact the Willow Creek Association at 1-800-570-9812. Or visit us on-line: www.willowcreek.com.

continue the transformation ...

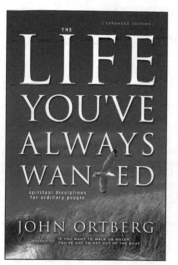

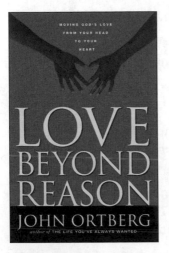

If You Want to Walk on Water, You've Got to Get Out of the Boat

JOHN ORTBERG

It's one thing to try to walk on water and sink some-times. But the real failure is to never get out of the boat.

We were made for something more than avoiding failure. As followers of Jesus, we want to go where he calls us. We want to step out in faith. But walk on water? What does that mean?

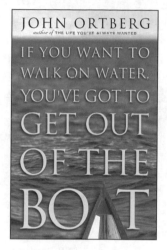

Walking on water means facing your fears and choosing not to let fear have the last word.

Walking on water means discovering and embracing the unique calling of God on your life.

Walking on water means experiencing the power of God in your life to do something you would not be capable of doing on your own.

John Ortberg, in his engaging and humorous style, reflects on this story in Matthew 14. He helps us recognize what boat we're in—the comfortable situation where we're hiding. He reminds us that there is a storm outside the boat—we will encounter problems. But if we're willing to get out of the boat, two things will happen. First, when we fail—and we will fail sometimes—Jesus will be there to pick us up. We will not fail alone. We will find he is wholly adequate to save us. And the second thing is, every once in a while, we'll walk on water! Because "if you want to walk on water, you've got to get out of the boat."

Hardcover: 0-310-22863-8

ZONDERVAN™

GRAND RAPIDS, MICHIGAN 49530 USA

WWW.ZONDERVAN.COM

Transform Your Church and Small Groups

Community 101
Gilbert Bilezikian

Written by one of Willow Creek's founders, this resource will help your church become a true community of believers. Bilezikian uses the Bible as his guide to demonstrate the centrality of community in God's plan of salvation and describe how it can be expressed in the daily life of the church.

Softcover – ISBN: 0-310-21741-5

Leading Life-Changing Small Groups
Bill Donahue and the Willow Creek Small Groups Team

Get the comprehensive guidance you need to cultivate life-changing small groups and growing, fruitful believers. Willow Creek's director of adult education and training shares in-depth the practical insights that have made Willow Creek's small group ministry so incredibly effective.

Softcover – ISBN: 0-310-24750-0

Available at your local bookstore!

ZONDERVAN™

GRAND RAPIDS, MICHIGAN 49530 USA

WWW.ZONDERVAN.COM

WILLOW

Willow Creek Resources

We want to hear from you. Please send your comments about this
book to us in care of zreview@zondervan.com. Thank you.

GRAND RAPIDS, MICHIGAN 49530 USA

ZONDERVAN.COM/
AUTHOR**TRACKER**